THE RIVER CAFÉ CLASSIC ITALIAN COOKBOOK

THE RIVER CAFÉ CLASSIC ITALIAN COOKBOOK

ROSE GRAY & RUTH ROGERS

PENGUIN
MICHAEL
JOSEPH

MICHAEL JOSEPH

Published by the Penguin Group
Penguin Books Ltd, 80 Strand, London WC2R 0RL, England
Penguin Group (USA) Inc., 375 Hudson Street, New York, New York 10014, USA
Penguin Group (Canada), 90 Eglinton Avenue East, Suite 700, Toronto, Ontario, Canada M4P 2Y3
(a division of Pearson Penguin Canada Inc.)
Penguin Ireland, 25 St Stephen's Green, Dublin 2, Ireland (a division of Penguin Books Ltd)
Penguin Group (Australia), 250 Camberwell Road, Camberwell, Victoria 3124, Australia
(a division of Pearson Australia Group Pty Ltd)
Penguin Books India Pvt Ltd, 11 Community Centre, Panchsheel Park,
New Delhi – 110 017, India
Penguin Group (NZ), 67 Apollo Drive, Rosedale, North Shore 0632, New Zealand
(a division of Pearson New Zealand Ltd)
Penguin Books (South Africa) (Pty) Ltd, 24 Sturdee Avenue,
Rosebank, Johannesburg 2196, South Africa

Penguin Books Ltd, Registered Offices: 80 Strand, London WC2R 0RL, England

www.penguin.com

First published 2009
1

Copyright © Rose Gray and Ruth Rogers, 2009

The moral right of the authors has been asserted

Printed in Italy by Printer Trento
Colour reproduction by Altaimage Ltd

A CIP catalogue record for this book is available from the British Library

ISBN: 978–0–718–15349–6

Photography copyright © 2009:
Giuseppe Bartolini: p50–51, p322–323, p348
Jonathan Gregson: p21, p35, p47, p59, p83, p93, p99, p155, p159, p177, p197, p203, p207,
p228, p229, p281, p282, p286, p297, p303, p311, p317, p345, p375
David Loftus: p15, p17, p25, p29, p53, p56(x4), p57, p61, p69, p71, p72, p75, p78, p106(x4),
p107(x4), p115, p119, p121, p128, p129, p133, p138, p141, p144, p145, p147, p153, p161,
p165, p168, p169, p171, p175, p178–179, p181, p183, p192, p193, p211, p215, p219, p237,
p240, p241, p245, p249, p251, p259, p265, p267, p273, p277, p293, p299, p300–301, p305,
p310, p321, p327, p335, p355, p357, p361, p362, p363, p367, p379, p387
Amedeo Novelli: p110–111, p224(x2), p225(x2), p370–371
Jean Pigozzi: p18–19, p87, p122, p148–149, p156–157, p172(x4), p173(x4), p194, p200,
p260–261, p287, p292, p338–339, p346
Mark Read: p30, p42(x4), p43(x4), p88–89, p94, p102–103, p186–187, p216, p232–233,
p268(x4), p314, p330–331, p332, p350–351, p380, p381, p388–389
Alan Rusbridger: p10–11, p22, p26, p36–37, p64–65, p79, p210, p254–55, p272, p306
Richard Bryant: p414-415

Designed by Mark Porter, assisted by Sarah Habershon
Jacket lettering by Peter Horridge
The River Café logo designed by David MacIlwaine

INTRODUCTION

We have had some extraordinary opportunities to visit Italy during the twenty–two years since we started the River Café. We love the architecture of the great cities, the landscapes, the sea and the mountains, but what we love most is the instinctive way food and wine play such an important part in everyday Italian life. From our very first visit, we have been inspired by the pride Italians take in their ingredients and their regional recipes. We knew then that this was the way we wanted to cook, and it is the way we still cook today.

We have travelled all over Italy, from Sicily to Piedmont, from Le Marche to Liguria, increasing our knowledge of the local specialities and classic recipes of each region. Through these journeys we have made friends with cooks, and have shared their passion for their family dishes – handed down from generation to generation. These talented people have taught us about the ingredients they use, and how to follow the seasons, using locally grown produce. Simple, regional cooking that gives endless pleasure – the Italian ethos. This book is the result of these encounters, which we want to share. It is our friendships with those who grow the grapes, tend the olive trees, make the wine and olive oil we use, the cheesemakers and salami producers, that have taught and inspired us.

The stallholders in the vegetable markets, whose produce changes throughout the year, have always explained to us the seasonality of what they grow and their way of making the most of what is abundant at any time. Eating in trattorias and people's homes has taught us, better than any elaborate research ever could, how to put a salad together using raw ovoli mushrooms and rocket in the summer, and how to make a soup with just three ingredients – broccoli, Lambrusco wine and garlic – in the winter.

Every recipe has its memories. We remember a visit to Giovanni Manetti, the famous wine and olive oil maker from Fontodi in Tuscany. His mother made us a ribollita, a soup of bread, cabbage and chicken stock that was unlike any Tuscan ribollita we had ever tasted because of its unusual sweet flavour. It made sense when we were told that she had changed the recipe in order to best show off her son's newly pressed, peppery, very green olive oil.

There was a winter's day we drove for miles up into the mountains of Piedmont behind Genoa to visit a wine dealer who wanted us to experience his grandmother's cooking. She and all the women of her family cooked for us the very delicious but frugal dishes they had

Most of what we have learnt
has been from Italians who
we've cooked with side by side.
With this book we want you
to cook side by side with us

survived on during the war. For three hours we sat with the men of the family in a vast, cold room, eating course after course of thick, creamy, comforting polenta, while the women stayed in the kitchen around the stove, stirring. This is where we learned how long polenta takes to cook. Every sauce we ate that day was made with wild ingredients – rabbits, hares, boar – with salads of wild herbs and greens.

On a trip to Puglia we slept in a bakery just so we could watch the many stages involved in the making of huge four–kilo semolina loaves throughout the night. We were astounded when we found out that these loaves used a sourdough 'mother' base that was started in 1945 and was still alive! We felt honoured to be given a piece of this 'mother' to take back to the River Café, and, since that trip, we use Pugliese bread every day.

In Maremma we were introduced to a winemaker whose estate makes a delicious Pecorino cheese. As we use fresh ricotta daily to stuff our ravioli, we were interested to see how they made their sheep's ricotta, the most delicate of all ricottas. Seeing it made, and tasting the soft warm curds by the teaspoonful that day, inspired us to use this cheese in various new ways.

On a more recent trip to Italy, we took the opportunity to visit Verona, a city we both love, to take photographs for this book. We returned to one of our favourite restaurants, Al Pompiere, for it was here, on our initial trip to VinItaly (the grand annual wine fair) in 1989, that we first ate risotto Amarone. The risotto was just as we remembered it from twenty years earlier – intensely flavoured with this powerful, spicy wine. When we make this risotto ourselves we use Mari Lisa Allegrini's Amarone, which we think is one of the best made in Valpolicella. Al Pompiere also specializes in local prosciutto and salami. There is lardo from Colonnata, local culatello, and the delicately soft sopressa, sweet horsemeat bresaola and mortadella. Every table is served large, carefully arranged platters of these meats, ranging in colour from pale pink to deep crimson, all prepared with great care by the chef, who presided over this domain with pride.

There are other restaurants in Italy that we always return to – Piperno in Rome for artichokes alla giudia, Alla Vecchia Bettola in Florence for arista di maiale, and, in Vernazza on the Ligurian coast, Trattoria Gianni Franzi for fritto misto and pesto. Every year in

November we go on a trip to Italy with our chefs from the River Café to choose a new olive oil and taste some wine. We always make a special detour to Scacciapensieri in Cecchina to visit the woman who bakes whole fish over potatoes. When we are in Piedmont in the white truffle season, we try to have a meal at Il Giardino da Felicin in Monforte d'Alba, which has an amazing view over the Barolo vineyards, and a beautiful cheese room. And in Milan we always try to discover a simple and surprising soup recipe at La Latteria.

This book is a collection and celebration of these wonderful Italian dishes. Inside you will find over 200 newly written recipes, the ones that we've been taught over the years and which mean so much to us, and those that we cook most often – our personal interpretation of these recipes and a tribute to the people we've met along the way.

This is classic Italian food – the traditional, regional food we love to eat when we are in Italy, the food we cook at the River Café, and the food we cook at home for our families.

Rose Gray and Ruth Rogers, 2009

SOUPS

SOUPS

Zuppa, passata, minestra, minestrina, crema, pappa and brodo are just some of the words Italians use to describe what we simply call 'soup'. Some of our favourite classic Italian soups are included in this chapter.

We find something very calming and creative about making a soup – the slow steps of building it up from the soffritto, adding the vegetables, beans, potatoes, the stock or water, and watching as the consistency, flavour and fragrance develop as it cooks.

The foundation of most soups is the soffritto, a lightly fried mixture of finely chopped vegetables and herbs. Traditionally, it consists of parsley, celery, garlic, carrots and onions, but pancetta, prosciutto or speck might also be added, or herbs such as thyme, sage and marjoram. We once watched a cook in Sardinia making a minestrone – she was surrounded by bowls of herbs, and added handfuls of each kind to the soffritto.

Broths or brodi are generally the basis for the soups of the north, like the one from the Val d'Aosta that we've included on page 32. They are light broths, achieved by simmering chicken, veal or beef with 'odori di cucina' – celery, carrots, onion and parsley – for about two hours. A flavourful vegetable broth, made by boiling carrots, celery, tomatoes, onions and herbs for about an hour, can be used as an alternative to traditional meat or chicken broth.

Italian bean soups can have subtle, complex flavours. When they are available, we use fresh cannellini or borlotti beans, which are harvested in the summer and are plentiful in all the markets in Italy, but dried ones are also delicious. Sometimes we use farro, barley and rice in place of beans.

In Tuscany, where bread is essential to cooking, it is almost always included in soups. The bread is unsalted and the texture is rough and grainy, with a thick crust. Traditionally bread was made once a week and, as it became hard and stale, thrifty Tuscan cooks developed recipes for soups such as ribollita and pappa al pomodoro – a summer soup fragrant with ripe tomatoes, basil and olive oil (see page 24). In the mountains of Piedmont, bread soups are filling and comforting, made with toasted bread placed in the bottom of a bowl, strong meat broths poured over, then covered with the local Fontina cheese.

When we were in Campagna, our winemaker friend Bruno Deconciliis was keen to introduce us to some of its unique ingredients. We visited an exceptional bakery that made freselle, a local traditional dry bread bun made with a fine-ground unbleached flour. In the restaurant Il Ceppo we ate a delicious zuppa alle vongole made with clams, garlic and chilli and a few torn-up late-season small tomatoes. No wine, no stock, but the freselle buns were there in the bowl to thicken the soup and were a crucial ingredient in giving it its particular texture and flavour.

Soup recipes can easily be adjusted to whatever ingredients you have to hand – as you make more and more soups you will become increasingly confident and find your own way. It takes time to understand Italian soups – how thick they can be, how they are often served at room temperature, the importance of olive oil and which ones taste better the next day. The ingredients in a soup can also tell you a lot about the area they originate from, the season you are in, the traditions of the area, and something about the person who cooked it.

ZUPPA CON SARDE

BORLOTTI AND SARDINE SOUP

Lipari is one of the beautiful Aeolian islands off Sicily. When we arrived we took a walk from the harbour up the hill and ate at Ristorante Filippino, sitting outside in the garden with views across the island and the sea. This soup is made with sardines, pine nuts and sultanas, ingredients used for the traditional Sicilian pasta sauce. To have them in this soup with borlotti beans was astonishing and memorable.

For 6

extra virgin olive oil

½ a red onion, peeled and finely sliced

3 salted anchovy fillets

1 tablespoon pine nuts, lightly toasted

1 tablespoon sultanas, soaked in hot water

2 garlic cloves, peeled: 1 finely chopped, 1 cut in half

1 tablespoon fennel seeds

12 whole sardines, filleted

sea salt and freshly ground black pepper

300g cooked borlotti beans (see page 307)

6 slices of ciabatta bread

2 tablespoons chopped fresh flat-leaf parsley

Heat 2 tablespoons of olive oil in a thick-bottomed saucepan. Add the onion and gently cook until soft and translucent but not brown. Add the anchovies and crush into the onion, then add the pine nuts, sultanas, chopped garlic and fennel seeds and stir to combine.

Lay the sardines in the pan and season them. Pour over just enough boiling water to cover the sardines, then cover and cook over a low heat for 5 minutes, or until the sardines are cooked. Add the borlotti beans and stir, crushing and breaking up the sardines.

Toast the bread and rub one side lightly with the halved garlic clove. Place each of these crostini in a bowl and ladle over the soup. Sprinkle with parsley and drizzle with extra virgin olive oil to serve.

ZUPPA ALLE VONGOLE

CLAM SOUP

Every Friday the fish sellers from Grosseto bring fish to the hill town of Montalcino. They sell from what is literally a hole in the walls of the town, but step inside and there is an abundance of glistening fresh fish – different sizes of squid, sea bass, swordfish, anchovies, clams and mussels. You have to get there early – and even then there is a queue – for by ten o'clock it is all gone. We bought clams and cooked them this way; the toast absorbs the delicious broth.

For 6

2kg small clams, washed

extra virgin olive oil

3 garlic cloves, peeled and finely chopped

2 dried red chillies, crumbled

3 tablespoons chopped fresh flat-leaf parsley, chopped

1 bottle of dry white wine, such as Vermentino

12 small slices of sourdough bread

Check over the clams and discard any that are not closed.

Heat 2 tablespoons of olive oil in a thick-bottomed saucepan large enough to hold the clams. Add all the garlic and chillies and half the parsley and cook for a few minutes. Add the wine, bring to the boil, cook for a minute, then add the clams. Stir well, to coat the clams with the wine. Cover the saucepan and cook the clams over a fairly high heat until they open, which will take 2 or 3 minutes. Discard any that remain closed.

Toast or grill the bread until brown, then prop up the pieces around the sides of a warmed oval dish. With a slotted spoon, remove the clams to the dish. Reduce the wine in the saucepan for a few minutes more, then pour over the clams.

Sprinkle over the remaining parsley and drizzle with plenty of extra virgin olive oil.

ZUPPA ALLE VONGOLE DI CAMPAGNA

A CLAM SOUP FROM CAMPAGNA

For 6

500g ripe vine cherry tomatoes
1 teaspoon fennel seeds, ground
sea salt and freshly ground black pepper
1 small light wholemeal loaf, with the bottom crust cut off
5 fresh red chillies
olive oil
4 garlic cloves, peeled and finely chopped
2kg small clams, washed
3 tablespoons chopped fresh flat-leaf parsley
extra virgin olive oil
1 lemon, juiced

Tear up the tomatoes and put them into a small bowl with all their juices. Add the ground fennel seeds. Season with sea salt and black pepper and leave to marinate for 45 minutes to an hour.

Preheat the oven to 110°C. Tear the bread into rough pieces the size of thick slices. Place on a rack and place in the oven to dry out, but not colour beyond a light tan. This should take 25–30 minutes.

Meanwhile check over the clams and discard any that are not closed. Cut the chillies in half lengthwise and scrape out most, but not all, of the seeds, then roughly chop. In a large thick-bottomed pan, gently heat 3 tablespoons of olive oil. Add the garlic, chilli and ½ a teaspoon of salt. When the garlic is soft and beginning to colour, turn up the heat and add the clams. Stir to turn the clams over in the oil, then add the tomatoes and their juice and 1 cup of water. Cover and cook until the clams have opened. Discard any that remain closed.

Throw in the parsley and test the juice for seasoning. Season with black pepper and add 2–3 tablespoons of extra virgin olive oil and the lemon juice.

Heat the soup bowls. Divide the dried bread between the bowls and pour over, in equal amounts, the clams and their juices. Remove any empty shells before serving.

We substitute the traditional freselle bread buns from Campagna with light wholemeal bread dried out in a low oven

ZUPPA DI BACCALÀ

DRIED COD SOUP

For 6

1 red onion, peeled and chopped
½ a celery head, chopped
3 garlic cloves, peeled and sliced
8 small potatoes, peeled and cut into 1cm cubes
3 bay leaves
2 dried red chillies, crumbled
freshly ground black pepper
8 plum tomatoes, drained of their juices if tinned
1kg dried cod stoccafisso, soaked and beaten (see page 176)
1 bottle of Pinot Bianco
1 lemon, juiced and zested
extra virgin olive oil
3 tablespoons finely chopped fresh flat-leaf parsley

Heat 3 tablespoons of olive oil in a thick-bottomed pan. Add the onion and celery and cook gently over a medium heat for about 10 minutes, until softened and lightly brown. Add half the garlic, the potatoes, bay leaves and chillies, season with black pepper and cook briefly to combine the flavours. Then add the tomatoes, breaking them up into the mixture. Cook, stirring to prevent sticking, over a low heat for about 35 minutes, until the potatoes are tender.

In a separate thick-bottomed pan heat 2 tablespoons of olive oil, add the rest of the garlic and, when it begins to colour, add the cod, skin side down. Pour in the wine to just cover the fish, add the lemon juice and cover the pan with a lid. Bring to the boil, then turn off the heat. If the cod is very thick you may have to simmer it for 5 minutes. Take the pan off the heat and leave, covered, for 10–15 minutes.

Remove the cod from the pan, break it up into pieces, removing the skin and bones, and add to the potatoes and tomatoes. Add the strained wine and juices from cooking the fish, stirring to combine. Test for seasoning; you may have to add salt!

Serve drizzled with extra virgin olive oil and with the parsley and lemon zest scattered over.

PAPPA AL POMODORO

BREAD AND TOMATO SOUP

Although we have always thought of pappa al pomodoro as a Tuscan soup, it is virtually unknown in the southern region of Tuscany. We discovered this one day when, having decided to make it, we asked a local cook how she did it and she suggested this method. After peeling the tomatoes, she put them into the food processor and made a thick purée.

It was delicious – we were lucky, as the tomatoes and the basil had been picked that morning and had a wonderful sweet flavour.

For 8

2kg very ripe tomatoes, peeled, skinned and deseeded

sea salt and freshly ground black pepper

200g stale bread, crusts removed, broken into pieces

a large bunch of fresh basil, leaves picked and torn

extra virgin olive oil

Roughly chop a quarter of the tomatoes and set aside. Place the rest in a food processor and blend until completely smooth and thick. Season well.

Put the blended mixture into a large pan and bring to the boil. Season generously, add the stale bread and stir until the bread absorbs the liquid and becomes soft. Add the chopped tomatoes and the basil leaves, stirring well. Check the seasoning again and drizzle with extra virgin olive oil.

This is a different version of pappa al pomodoro – we used the purée as the base of the soup, though we peeled and chopped some more tomatoes to stir through just at the end of cooking

MINESTRONE ESTIVO

SUMMER MINESTRONE

In a small trattoria just inside the Italian border not far from Ventimiglia, they serve bowls of minestrone at each table setting, a refreshing way to begin a summer lunch as an alternative to pasta.

For 6

2 tablespoons extra virgin olive oil

1 red onion, peeled and finely sliced

1.5kg very young peas, podded

2 medium potatoes, peeled and cut in 0.5cm thick slices

a bunch of fresh mint, leaves picked, stalks kept, plus 3 tablespoons chopped fresh mint for serving

2 litres water or chicken stock

3kg very young broad beans, podded

sea salt and freshly ground black pepper

Heat the olive oil in a thick-bottomed pan and gently fry the onion for about 5 minutes, until soft and translucent. Add the peas and potatoes and cook, stirring frequently, for 5 minutes, then add a handful of the mint leaves. Pour in enough water or stock to cover, and simmer for 10 minutes. Add half the broad beans and simmer for 5 minutes more.

Bring a large pan of salted water to the boil and add the mint stalks and the remaining broad beans. Cook, covered, for 2–3 minutes, then drain, discarding the mint stalks.

Put a ladleful of the soup mixture into a food processor with a ladleful of blanched broad beans, and pulse-blend to a rough texture. Remove from the processor and keep to one side. Pulse-blend the remainder of the soup with the rest of the mint leaves. Return the soup to the pan and add the remaining whole broad beans and the puréed broad bean mixture. Season well with salt and pepper.

Serve the soup at room temperature, sprinkled with the chopped fresh mint. The soup should be very thick, with a combination of whole young broad beans and a rough purée. It is also delicious with a dollop of fresh pesto (see page 399) on each serving.

ZUPPA DI PANE

BREAD SOUP

We have been making ribollita for so long that it was interesting to discover another type of vegetable, bean and bread soup. Zuppa di pane has no soffritto but has the addition of potatoes. The vegetables are boiled in water, imparting their flavour to the broth.

For 8

extra virgin olive oil

1 red onion, peeled and finely sliced

2 garlic cloves, peeled and chopped

6 large waxy potatoes, peeled and quartered

2 plum tomatoes, coarsely chopped

1 head of celery, all green parts removed, coarsely chopped

2 zucchini, roughly chopped

200g cooked fresh or dried cannellini or borlotti beans (see pages 307–8)

1.5kg green chard, roughly chopped including stalks

200g very stale white bread, crusts removed, torn into small pieces

In a large thick-bottomed pan, heat 2 tablespoons of olive oil. Lightly brown the onion and garlic for a few minutes, then add the potatoes, tomatoes, celery and zucchini. Stir to combine and cook for 5 minutes.

Add the beans if using fresh ones. Cover very generously with water, bring to the boil and cook for 30 minutes, then add the chard and stalks and cook for another hour. The stock will be a dark colour. If using cooked dried cannellini beans, add them now and cook for a further 15 minutes.

Put the stale bread into a large soup bowl and pour the soup over. Stir to combine – the bread will absorb most of the liquid and become soft. Check the seasoning and add some extra virgin olive oil. Let the soup sit for half an hour to cool and intensify the flavours.

Serve at room temperature, drizzled with extra virgin olive oil.

Soups in Italy vary not only from
region to region but from village to village

ACQUA COTTA

BREAD AND TOMATO SOUP WITH PORCINI

We first ate this in the restaurant Due Peppe in Saturnia, driving from Orvieto to the Maremma. Acqua cotta, translated as 'cooked water', belies its simple name. It is one of the most sophisticated Tuscan soups, using dried porcini mushrooms, ripe tomatoes and toasted Tuscan bread. It is important to cook the soffritto of carrots, onion, celery and garlic for a long time – until they become soft, lose their individual shape and merge into one strong flavour.

For 6

75g dried porcini mushrooms
extra virgin olive oil
1 medium onion, peeled and finely chopped
2 carrots, peeled and roughly chopped
1 celery heart with leaves, finely chopped
4 garlic cloves, peeled: 3 chopped, 1 cut in half
2 tablespoons chopped fresh flat-leaf parsley
1 small dried chilli, crumbled
1 x 850g tin of peeled plum tomatoes
sea salt and freshly ground black pepper
6 slices of ciabatta bread, cut into 1.5cm thick slices

Soak the porcini in a bowl of lukewarm water for an hour.

Heat 3 tablespoons of extra virgin olive oil in a large, thick-bottomed pan and gently fry the onion, carrots, celery, chopped garlic, parsley and chilli until soft.

Drain the porcini, reserving the soaking liquid, then rinse and roughly chop. Add to the cooked vegetables and cook gently for a further 5 minutes, or until soft. Add the tomatoes to the pan, smashing them into the mixture one by one. Season.

Cook for about 45 minutes to 1 hour, adding some of the strained reserved mushroom liquid, and a small amount of hot water if necessary. Acqua cotta is a very thick soup. Season well.

Grill the slices of bread on both sides and rub one side with the halved garlic clove. Place a toast in each bowl and cover with a ladleful of soup. Drizzle with extra virgin olive oil.

ZUPPA D'AOSTA

CABBAGE AND FONTINA SOUP FROM VAL D'AOSTA

Val d'Aosta is the most Alpine of the Italian provinces and its proximity to France has influenced its cooking. In this soup the combination of Fontina, a mountain cheese, with anchovies and bread, expresses all those influences. In the past the people here traded their dairy produce for salted anchovies from the coast, and cabbage was a vegetable they could grow easily.

For 6
1 Savoy cabbage
1 ciabatta loaf, or ½ a Pugliese loaf, crusts removed
1 garlic clove, peeled and cut in half
1 litre chicken stock
sea salt and freshly ground black pepper
50g unsalted butter
120g Fontina, coarsely grated
12 salted anchovy fillets, plus extra for finishing
50g Parmesan, finely grated, plus extra for serving

Preheat the oven to 180°C. Remove the leaves from the cabbage one by one, and cut out the thick stems from the centre of each leaf, keeping the leaves whole. Use the dark green outer leaves and bright green inner leaves – keep the central paler leaves for a different recipe. Bring a large pan of salted water to the boil. Blanch the cabbage leaves until tender; this will take up to 5 minutes, especially for the tougher outer leaves, which have the most interesting flavour. Drain, set aside and keep warm. Cut the bread into 1cm thick slices and toast on each side. Rub one side lightly with the garlic. Bring the stock to the boil and test for seasoning. Leave on a very low heat.

Butter the base of a medium thick-bottomed casserole and put in a layer of cabbage leaves, sprinkled with a little salt and pepper. Cover the cabbage with a layer of grated Fontina and a layer of toast. Place 4 anchovy fillets over the toast, dot with butter, then cover with two further layers of cabbage leaves, Fontina, toast and anchovies. Finish with a layer of cabbage, Fontina and a few anchovies. Dot with butter and sprinkle the Parmesan on top. The layers should only come two-thirds of the way up the casserole.

Slowly pour in the hot stock. Place in the oven for 30 minutes, and bake until the cheese has melted into a golden crust. Cut the soup out of the casserole into warm bowls, using a large kitchen spoon. This is a very substantial soup that is a meal in itself. Serve with Parmesan.

ZUPPA DI CANNELLINI

CANNELLINI SOUP WITH PORCINI

This is a very thick substantial soup from Atripalda in Avellino, the mountainous area on the coast south of Naples famous for its wine. It was made for us in the late summer last year when fresh cannellini beans, plum tomatoes and porcini mushrooms were all in season. The flavour from the uncooked porcini, slightly warmed by the beans, is unusually delicious and very simple to achieve. You can substitute zolfino beans for cannellini.

For 6

600g fresh cannellini beans in their pods, or 200g dried white cannellini beans soaked overnight and cooked (see page 308)

2 garlic cloves, peeled and kept whole

3 large ripe tomatoes, washed

1 large sprig of fresh sage, leaves picked

extra virgin olive oil

500g fresh porcini mushrooms

sea salt and freshly ground black pepper

2 tablespoons fresh oregano leaves, chopped

Pod the fresh beans, wash and drain, then place in a large, thick-bottomed pan. Cover with cold water and add the garlic, whole tomatoes, sage and 3 tablespoons of extra virgin olive oil. Bring to the boil, then turn down the heat and simmer very gently, half covering the saucepan, until the beans are tender, about 30–40 minutes. Remove from the heat and keep warm.

Clean the porcini caps by wiping them with a damp cloth. Scrape the stems with a small knife and cut off any rotten bits. Cut the caps into fine slices and roughly chop the stalks.

Drain the cooking water from the beans and keep it to one side. Use a potato masher or fork and smash the tomatoes, garlic and most of the beans together in the pan, keeping the texture quite rough but keeping some of the beans whole. Season.

Put the beans back on to a medium heat and add the porcini stalks, stirring to mix them into the beans. Add enough of the reserved bean water to loosen the consistency to a thick cream and bring to the boil. Finally stir in the porcini caps.

Take the soup off the heat and check for seasoning. When ready to serve, sprinkle over the oregano and drizzle with extra virgin olive oil.

CAVOLO NERO SOUP WITH POLENTA

There are many recipes around northern Tuscany for farinata, the regional name for soup made with polenta and cavolo nero. It is picked as the first frosts arrive, when the flavour of the cabbage is sweet and the texture creamy. Tuscans love to pour lots of their wonderful, green, peppery, newly pressed olive oil over this soup. We first ate farinata at Cappezzana, a wine and olive oil producing estate in Carmignano, near Florence.

For 6–8
olive oil
1 red onion, peeled and chopped
1 celery head, centre white part and leaves roughly chopped
2 carrots, peeled and diced
2 medium potatoes, peeled and diced
2 garlic cloves, peeled and sliced
1 tablespoon fresh sage leaves, roughly chopped
1 tablespoon fresh rosemary leaves, roughly chopped
1 dried red chilli, crumbled
1kg cavolo nero leaves, washed and centre stems stripped off, roughly chopped
250g coarse polenta flour
sea salt and freshly ground black pepper
extra virgin olive oil

Heat 4 tablespoons of olive oil in a thick-bottomed pan, add the onion, celery stalks and carrot, and cook until the onion is turning brown and all the vegetables are soft. Add the potatoes, garlic, sage, rosemary and chilli, and cook, stirring, for just a few minutes. Add the cavolo nero, then just cover it with water and add 2 tablespoons of olive oil. Bring to the boil, then turn down the heat and simmer gently for an hour. The soup should be watery, not too thick.

Now add the polenta in a thin stream (pour it from a jug to control the amount), simmering and stirring all the time with a wooden spoon. The soup will thicken very quickly when you first add the polenta – add more hot water if you feel it is too thick. Cook until the polenta is soft, which will take at least 30 minutes. Season and serve with the freshest new season's extra virgin olive oil.

Farinata is found on menus
from the end of October to Christmas

PASTA & GNOCCHI

PASTA & GNOCCHI

In the Italian menu, pasta or gnocchi are served after the antipasti course and before the secondo. Seen as dishes to stimulate the appetite, they therefore come in rather small portions – the perfect amount should leave you not too full to enjoy the rest of the meal. When we travel through Italy we always know where we are by the pasta we eat, for every region – indeed almost every city – has its own particular type.

Emilia Romagna is the home of fresh pasta, and in Bologna, Modena and Parma making pasta is part of daily life. Using fresh golden yellow 'rossi' egg yolks and Tipo '00 ' flour, 'pasta all'uova fatta in casa' is rolled out and either folded around delicate fillings to create the traditional stuffed pastas such as ravioli, tortellini and agnolotti, or cut into various widths of ribbons: tagliatelle, the fine tagliarini or the very wide pappardelle.

Making fresh pasta is one of the most pleasurable of cooking experiences, particularly if you have a special ingredient – when you have delicious fresh ricotta to use in a stuffed pasta like ravioli; or in the summer, when you have the most perfect pungent basil for pesto and you want to enjoy it with the fresh thin Ligurian lasagnette; or if you are fortunate enough to have a white truffle to slice over delicate fine egg tagliarini. There is not just one recipe or technique for making fresh egg pasta. Talking to cooks in Liguria and Piedmont, we have learned their many recipes and developed the ones we think are the most delicate and fine-flavoured. If you find you don't have enough time to make your own, or don't have a pasta machine, we think it is better to buy a superior dried egg pasta than to use commercially manufactured fresh pasta.

It is dried pasta that most Italians cook and eat every day. The best is made from 100% durum wheat, the hardest wheat grain. In Rome, it is the basis for well-known dishes such as spaghettini aglio, olio e peperoncino, with olive oil, garlic and dried chilli; spaghetti alla carbonara, made with eggs, pancetta and Parmesan; and bucatini all'amatriciana.

Bucatini are like thick spaghetti but with a hole down the centre, and are perfect for the strong-flavoured sauce of pancetta, onion and tomato. In Naples local pastas include conchiglie (shells) which hold small clams and their juices. In Puglia the orecchiette (little ears) are perfect for cime di rapa (turnip tops) in a thick anchovy sauce. In Lucca and Florence, larger pasta quills of penne lisce (smooth) or rigate (ridged) are served with spicy arrabbiata sauce, or with stracotto, a rich dark sauce made from cooking a whole piece of beef in wine until it melts and becomes the sauce itself.

We have also included recipes for gnocchi in this chapter, the dumplings traditionally made in northern Italy. For us, the gnocchi we like best are made simply with potatoes and flour, but they can also be made with spinach and ricotta, or squash (see page 54). The less you handle the dough and the less flour you use, the lighter the gnocchi will be.

Whether it's fresh or dried pasta that you are going to cook, there are certain guidelines that we recommend you follow. Use a large thick-bottomed pan and a generous amount of water. Have a colander ready in the sink for draining, or, the method we prefer, tongs or a spider next to the pot to remove the pasta straight to the sauce. Add salt to the water when it has boiled and then bring it back to the boil. Submerge the pasta completely and stir it with a fork to separate the strands. Taste the pasta before the cooking time indicated on the packet – it should be al dente (firm to the bite, but with no white in the middle when it is broken) – and be aware that pasta continues to cook after draining until it cools down. When draining the pasta, leave a little of the cooking water clinging so that it is glossy with moisture. Keep back a small amount of the cooking water for loosening the sauce after combining with the pasta if it seems too thick. Toss the pasta a few times to thoroughly distribute the sauce. Grate the cheese just before serving and eat the pasta immediately. Always have your plates hot and your guests waiting at the table.

PASTA FRESCA

BASIC EGG PASTA

Makes approximately 1kg, to serve 6

500g Tipo '00' flour, plus extra for dusting

1 teaspoon sea salt

4 large free-range organic eggs

6 large free-range organic egg yolks

50g fine semolina flour, for dusting

Put the flour and salt into a food processor, add the eggs and egg yolks, and pulse-blend with a dough hook until the pasta begins to come together into a loose ball of dough. Knead the dough on a flat surface, lightly dusted with semolina and a little extra flour, for about 3 minutes, until smooth. If it is very stiff and difficult to knead, you may have to put it back into the processor and blend in another whole egg. Cut the dough into 8 equal-sized pieces and briefly knead into individual balls. Wrap in clingfilm and allow to rest in the fridge for at least 20 minutes.

Set your pasta machine on the widest setting. Flour the work surface and push each piece of dough through the rollers 10 times, folding the sheet into 3 each time, then turning it by a quarter and pushing it through the rollers again. This introduces air into the dough and stretches it to develop the texture. After 10 folds the pasta should feel silky. Only then reduce the setting gradually down to thin, as required. You should achieve long sheets; cut them in half if they become too long to handle.

To cut tagliatelle, dust the sheets with flour and while they're still pliable fold each one loosely over and over again on itself until the whole sheet has been folded into a long, flat, rectangular roll 8cm wide. Using a wide-bladed knife, cut the roll across into ribbons, using both your hands with your fingers apart to lift and separate the ribbon rolls. Alternatively, if you have a cutter on your machine, put the pasta through the widest measure. Make sure your surface is generously scattered with flour, and separate the ribbons as they emerge from the machine.

Always cook fresh pasta in a large thick-bottomed saucepan three-quarters full of water to which you have added 1–2 teaspoons of sea salt. Cooking times will vary according to the thickness of the pasta ribbons – those made from this recipe will normally take 3–4 minutes to cook. Fresh pasta should have hardly any bite but should never be soft, i.e. overcooked. We always allow for the minute of extra cooking when you combine the pasta with the sauce after you have taken it out of the water.

PASTA VERDE

BASIC SPINACH EGG PASTA

In Ligurian grocery shops you can buy cooked spinach squeezed into egg-sized balls, as there is a strong tradition for making fresh pasta in nearly every household. The spinach replaces half the eggs in the pasta dough mixture.

Makes approximately 1kg, to serve 6

500g spinach, washed, tough stalks removed

500g Tipo '00' flour, plus extra for dusting

1 teaspoon sea salt

2 large free-range organic eggs

2 large free-range organic egg yolks

Boil the spinach in a large pan of salted water for about 5 minutes, until soft. Drain in a colander, then place on kitchen paper and press hard until almost dry. Chop the spinach roughly, then gather up and shape into 2 balls the same size as the eggs.

Put the flour and salt into a food processor fitted with a dough hook. Add the eggs and yolks and the spinach and pulse-blend until the dough comes together and is a solid green colour. If the dough is too soft, add extra flour when kneading to stiffen it up. Remove it to a floured surface and knead with your hands for about 5 minutes until it feels smooth and silky. Wrap in clingfilm and place in the fridge for a minimum of 1 hour.

Set your pasta machine on the widest setting. Flour the work surface and push each piece of dough through the rollers 10 times, folding the sheet into 3 each time, then turning it by a quarter and pushing it through the rollers again. This process introduces air into the dough and stretches it to develop the texture. After 10 folds the pasta should feel silky. Only then reduce the setting gradually down to thin, as required. You should achieve long sheets; cut them in half if they become too long to handle. To cut the pasta into pappardelle, scatter a little flour over the pasta and your work surface, then cut the sheets of dough into 3–4cm wide ribbons. Divide the ribbons into 6 and loosely gather them together.

If making the pappardelle by hand, knead the dough for at least 30 minutes, then roll it out as thin as you can. Working fresh pasta should be done in a cool place to prevent the dough from drying out. Pappardelle can be made up to 2 days in advance so long as you keep it covered. Any leftover pasta should be completely dried, then kept in an airtight container. To cook, see opposite.

Making egg pasta by hand in Trattoria Caprini in Verona

PASTA LIGURE

FRESH PASTA WITH WINE FROM LIGURIA

This is the pasta to make for lasagnette di Laura on page 48.

Makes approximately 1kg, to serve 6	
500g Tipo '00' pasta flour, plus extra for dusting	
1 large free-range organic egg	
3 large free-range organic egg yolks	
50ml white wine	
2 tablespoons extra virgin olive oil	
1 teaspoon sea salt	

Sieve the flour into the bowl of a food processor fitted with a dough hook. Add the eggs, wine, olive oil and salt. Knead slowly, allowing the mixture to come together. Keep the processor on a low speed and knead for 10 minutes. The dough should be quite dry.

Dust your work surface with plenty of flour. Divide the dough into 4 pieces and work each piece by hand until completely smooth. Wrap each ball of dough in clingfilm and put into the fridge to chill for 1½–2 hours.

Prepare your pasta machine, setting it on the widest setting. Scatter the work surface with more flour and push each piece of dough through the rollers 10 times, folding the sheet into 3 each time to return it to a short strip, then turning it by a quarter and pushing it through the rollers again. This process introduces air into the dough and stretches it to develop the texture. After 10 folds at this setting the pasta should feel silky. Only then reduce the setting gradually down to thin, as required. You should achieve long sheets; cut them in half if you find they become too long to handle.

Try to roll this pasta as thin as your machine will go — the sheets should be almost transparent. Cut the sheets into ribbons when still freshly rolled, and use as quickly as possible. This pasta cooks in 3 minutes and is commonly used with pesto (see page 399).

PASTA PIEMONTESE

RICH EGG PASTA FROM PIEDMONT

This is the pasta to make for taglierini with white truffles on page 46.

Makes approximately 1kg, to serve 6

500g Tipo '00' pasta flour, plus extra for dusting

20 large free-range organic egg yolks

1 tablespoon sea salt

Put the main quantity of flour into the bowl of a food processor fitted with a dough hook, then add the egg yolks and salt. Mix slowly for about 10 minutes to knead to a dough. Remove from the processor, wrap in clingfilm, and leave to cool and rest for 1 hour.

Prepare your pasta machine, setting it on the widest setting. Scatter the work surface with flour and push each piece of dough through the rollers 10 times, folding the sheet into 3 each time to return it to a short strip, then turning it by a quarter and pushing it through the rollers again. This process introduces air into the dough and stretches it to develop the texture. After 10 folds at this setting the pasta should feel silky. Only then reduce the setting gradually down to thin, as required. You should achieve long sheets; cut them in half if you find they become too long to handle.

Fold the pasta sheets over three or four times back on themselves, then cut the pile as finely as you can into tagliarini, 2–3mm wide. Toss the cut tagliarini to loosen and lightly coat with flour. Use as soon as possible – to cook, see basic egg pasta (page 40).

TAGLIERINI AL TARTUFO

TAGLIERINI WITH WHITE TRUFFLES

This is a dish for a very special occasion, as white truffles are the most expensive ingredient in the Italian larder. The season is very short, usually starting some time in October and finishing at the end of December. White truffles are unique among fungi, as their pungent aroma overwhelms you even more than their taste. The price varies enormously, as can the quality. A good truffle should be firm to touch and have a good strong smell. People often say you should store a white truffle in rice or among eggs, but if you do this the rice and eggs will absorb the flavour. We wrap them in very light kitchen paper or paper table napkins, slightly moistened, and put them in a sealed box on the lowest shelf or inside the door of the fridge. Always use a sharp truffle slicer, as fine shavings are vital to break the tiny cells in the truffle which contain the flavour.

Since we wrote the first River Café cookbook, our experience and knowledge of truffles has expanded. We learnt the method of cleaning truffles used here from Giuseppe Boggione, who was the first truffle-hunter to share his skills with us. This was in the village of Monforte d'Alba in Piedmont, after our successful hunt, when he cleaned the truffles in the village fountain with a toothbrush he kept in his jacket pocket. Later we ate them shaved over our breakfast eggs.

For 4
10g fresh white truffle
250g dried Italian-made taglierini, or fresh rich egg pasta (see page 45)
sea salt and freshly ground black pepper
20g unsalted butter
½ a nutmeg, freshly grated (optional)

Clean the truffle; we use a wet toothbrush and very gently brush the surface to remove any clay or sand that may be stuck in the crevices. Wipe the truffle dry. Make sure you have a sharp truffle slicer, as truffles are quite brittle and will easily break and crumble.

Cook the taglierini in boiling salted water until al dente. Melt the butter until just soft, adding a pinch of nutmeg and black pepper and a few shavings of truffle. Drain the pasta, keeping back 2–3 tablespoons of the cooking water. Add the pasta to the warm butter mixture and toss to coat each strand. Serve on hot plates and grate the truffle generously over each.

LASAGNETTE DI LAURA

PASTA SILK HANDKERCHIEFS WITH PESTO

We were staying near Portofino, researching the food of Liguria, when someone told us about Da Laura. It has since become one of our favourite restaurants. The only way to get there is by boat or a two-hour hike from Portofino. People come from all over to eat their lasagnette, transparent sheets of pasta layered with a bright green, delicate pesto – they buy the sheets ready-made from Fiorella, the fresh pasta shop in Camogli.

For 6

½ x quantity Ligurian pasta dough (see page 44)

1 x quantity pesto (see page 399)

extra virgin olive oil

50g Parmesan, freshly grated

Dust a work surface with plenty of flour. Divide the pasta dough into 4 pieces and work each piece by hand until completely smooth. Wrap each ball of dough in clingfilm and put into the fridge to chill for 1½–2 hours.

To prepare the final stage of the dough, use a pasta machine. Put each ball of dough through the widest setting 10 times, folding the thick sheet into 3 as it emerges to form a short, very thick piece. Turn this around, and put it through the machine again. Keeping the machine on this setting, repeat this process until the pasta feels silky. Only then reduce the setting gradually down to a fine pasta sheet. When you have the pasta on its finest setting, cut it into 8–10cm squares.

Cook these 'handkerchiefs' a few at a time in boiling salted water until al dente – about 2 minutes. Remove with a slotted spoon. To serve, spread a small amount of pesto on to each warm plate, arrange 3 or 4 sheets of pasta on top, and place another small amount of pesto on top of the pasta. Drizzle with extra virgin olive oil and serve with the Parmesan.

TAGLIATELLE CON PORCINI

TAGLIATELLE WITH DRIED PORCINI AND SAGE

There is a huge variation in the dried porcini mushrooms available. Drying deprives the mushrooms of their succulence but intensifies their flavour, making them an excellent ingredient for pasta sauces. Look for large, creamy, tanned slices with a delicate mushroom perfume, and avoid packets containing dark crumbly ones. The price varies and, on the whole, the more expensive the better the quality. Once the packet is open, store in a jar with a tight-fitting lid. The soaking water is full of flavour and should always be used in this recipe.

For 4
75g dried porcini
rind of 1 lemon
100g unsalted butter
2 garlic cloves, peeled and finely sliced
10 fresh sage leaves, washed and roughly chopped
1 dried chilli, crumbled
100ml double cream
sea salt and freshly ground black pepper
320g dried egg tagliatelle, or $2/3$ x quantity basic egg pasta dough (see page 40)
50g Parmesan, freshly grated

Soak the porcini in 450ml of hot water for 20 minutes. Cut the lemon rind into fine strips. Drain the porcini, reserving the water. Rinse and roughly chop. Strain the liquid through a sieve lined with muslin.

Melt the butter in a thick-bottomed pan and add the garlic, sage and chilli. Cook for about 5 minutes, until lightly coloured, then add the porcini. Continue to fry until soft, then add the porcini liquid and simmer for about a minute, until most of the juice has been absorbed. Add the cream and the lemon rind, and reduce until the sauce is creamy and thick. Season.

Cook the dried tagliatelle in boiling salted water for about 8–10 minutes, until al dente (fresh will take less time), and drain. Add to the sauce, turning the pasta over to coat each ribbon. Serve in warm bowls, with Parmesan on the side.

Da Laura is literally a shack on a crowded beach with one oven and four burners, and chairs and tables on the sand

GNOCCHI DI PATATE

POTATO GNOCCHI

For 6

1kg white floury potatoes, medium to large

100g plain flour

sea salt and freshly ground black pepper

1 large free-range organic egg, beaten lightly

extra virgin olive oil or salted butter

Wash the potatoes, taking care not to break the skin and keeping them whole.

Bring a large pan of salted water to the boil. Add the potatoes and boil until soft – this will take about 20–25 minutes, according to their size. Drain and peel the potatoes while still hot and immediately put through a mouli or potato ricer on to a flat, clean surface.

Sift the flour over the warm potato and scatter over 1 tablespoon of sea salt and ½ teaspoon of black pepper. Make a well in the centre, add the beaten egg and use your hands to rapidly form a smooth, soft dough. Do not overwork the dough or you will make the gnocchi too dense. Divide the dough into four.

Roll the dough into sausage-shaped lengths of 1.5cm diameter and cut these into pieces 2.5cm long. To form the gnocchi, press each piece against the prongs of a fork to make little ridges on one side. This shape holds the sauce you choose to serve with the gnocchi.

Cook batches of the gnocchi in boiling salted water for 3 minutes, or until they rise to the surface. Taste one of the gnocchi to make sure they are cooked through, then remove with a slotted spoon to a warmed dish and toss in a little extra virgin olive oil or salted butter.

Potato gnocchi can be served simply tossed with extra virgin olive oil and Parmesan, or with a rich tomato sauce such as the one on page 397.

We like to use Desiree potatoes
for making potato gnocchi

GNOCCHI DI ZUCCA

POTATO AND PUMPKIN GNOCCHI

Pumpkin gnocchi are a variation on potato gnocchi (see page 52). Pumpkin is very often used in northern Italian cooking as a filling for stuffed pasta such as ravioli and panzotti. In this recipe, it gives a delicate and interesting flavour when mixed with potato and needs only a sauce of melted butter with sage leaves.

For 4

800g floury potatoes

500g pumpkin or delicate squash

extra virgin olive oil

2 dried red chillies, crumbled

1 teaspoon dried oregano

sea salt and freshly ground black pepper

2 large free-range organic eggs, beaten

200g plain flour, plus extra for rolling

50g Parmesan

In a large pan of salted water, boil the potatoes for about 30 minutes with their skins on. When cooked, drain, peel and put them through a ricer or mouli while still warm.

Preheat the oven to 180°C. Peel the pumpkin or squash, slice in half lengthways and remove the seeds. Cut into 3–4cm cubes and toss in a bowl with just enough extra virgin olive oil to coat the pieces lightly. Add the chillies and oregano and season.

Line a baking tray with parchment and lay the pumpkin on top. Cover with another layer of parchment and bake in the oven until soft, about 30 minutes. Put through a mouli or potato ricer and add to the potatoes, stirring to combine. Place the mixture in a mound on a clean work surface. Make a crater in the middle, pour in the eggs and season.

Knead the mixture with your hands, adding the flour a little at a time. It is essential to work the dough quickly, as the longer it is worked, the heavier the gnocchi become.

Lightly dust a work surface with flour. Shape the dough into several long rolls about 1.5cm in diameter. Cut each roll into 2cm pieces. The gnocchi can be pressed with your fingers, or a fork, or may be left as they are.

Bring a large pan of salted water to the boil. Gently lower the gnocchi, a dozen or so at a time, into the boiling water. Stir gently until they rise to the surface, to keep them from sticking together. The total cooking time will be about 3 minutes. Remove the gnocchi with a slotted spoon, drain, and transfer to a warm serving plate. Repeat until all the gnocchi are cooked, and serve with extra virgin olive oil drizzled over and Parmesan sprinkled on top.

MALFATTI DI BIETOLA

MALFATTI OF SWISS CHARD

The Italian word 'malfatti', literally translated, means 'badly made'. In Campagna the word describes the broken and irregular pieces of the dried hard wheat pasta that is formed in many shapes and sizes and often sold off cheaply to be used in soups.

We use Swiss chard leaves in our recipe, though some cooks choose to use spinach. In Tuscany, fresh ricotta will always be sheep's ricotta, but buffalo ricotta, when we can get hold of it, works very well, otherwise we use fresh cow's ricotta.

For 8–10

1kg Swiss chard leaves
500g fresh ricotta
4 large free-range organic eggs
¼ of a nutmeg, freshly grated
50g Parmesan, plus extra for serving
sea salt and freshly ground black pepper
3 tablespoons Tipo '00' flour, plus extra for dusting
200g fine semolina flour
250g unsalted butter, softened
a small bunch of fresh sage, leaves picked

Cut the stalks from the chard leaves and discard, and wash the leaves well. Bring a large saucepan of salted water to the boil and cook the leaves for 5 minutes, or until soft. Drain, squeezing every bit of water out. Chop finely and let cool. Beat the ricotta with a fork and add the chopped chard. Add the eggs, nutmeg and Parmesan and season. Fold in the flour and dust a tray with more flour.

Take a wine glass and dust it with semolina. Put a dessertspoon of the ricotta/chard mixture into the glass and swill it around until a shape is formed. The malfatti must be well coated with the semolina. Place them on the floured tray.

Heat a serving dish with a knob of butter. Bring a large pan of salted water to the boil. Drop in the malfatti in batches and cook until they float. This will take about 5 minutes. Remove with a slotted spoon and place in the warmed dish. Keep warm while you cook the rest.

Slowly melt the remaining butter in a thick-bottomed pan over a low heat; add the sage leaves and just let them wilt and blend into the butter. Serve the malfatti with the sage butter and Parmesan.

These loosely shaped gnocchi are formed in a wine glass by swirling the soft dough pieces inside the glass, the same gesture one would use when releasing the perfumes of wine

GNUDI BIANCHI

RICOTTA GNOCCHI IN SEMOLINA FLOUR

We were introduced to gnudi at a restaurant called Da Marino in Vinci, close to Florence. The cook there taught us the recipe and it has been on the menu at the River Café ever since. In November we like to pour the green peppery extra virgin olive oil, the just pressed stuff, over the gnudi. Make the gnudi 24 hours before you want to cook them, to allow the semolina to stick to the surface to form a fine coating.

For 4

500g ricotta (sheep's if possible, but cow's is good too)

½ a nutmeg, freshly grated

100g Parmesan, grated, plus extra for serving

sea salt and freshly ground white pepper

500g semolina flour

extra virgin olive oil

Strain the ricotta in a sieve until no more liquid comes out. Put it into a bowl and beat it with a fork until it becomes light and fluffy. Grate in the nutmeg and stir, then stir in the Parmesan. Season the mixture generously. Put it into the fridge for 30 minutes.

Put half the semolina on to a flat tray so that it covers the surface. Generously dust the remaining semolina over a large, clean work surface.

Take a large spoonful of the ricotta mixture and roll it into a short sausage 1.5cm thick, then cut into 2cm pieces. Gently form these pieces into balls, coat them with the semolina from the work surface, and place them on the tray. Repeat this process until all the ricotta mixture is used up. When you have finished making all the gnudi, add them to the semolina in the tray and shake well so that they are almost submerged. Put into the fridge for 24 hours.

Cook the gnudi in a large pan of boiling salted water for 3 minutes, or until they rise to the surface. Remove with a slotted spoon to a warmed dish and serve with Tuscan extra virgin olive oil.

Eat gnudi steaming hot and
the astonishing flavours of fresh
ricotta, hints of nutmeg
and salty Parmesan are a delight

PAPPARDELLE ALLA LEPRE

PAPPARDELLE WITH HARE SAUCE

Using game to make meat sauces is an important part of Tuscan cuisine. In Lucca, years ago, we learnt from cooks how they used spices and cream to enrich these sauces, and how to make them go further by including cheese and tomatoes. In most restaurants the texture of the finished sauce will be quite fine but that is the choice of individual cooks – here we have kept the sauce quite meaty and dark, a rich, spicy recipe that you may want to follow with a light secondo.

For 6

1 whole hare, including liver, kidneys and heart

For the marinade

1 bottle of Chianti Classico

1 cinnamon stick

50g juniper berries

1 teaspoon black peppercorns

2 dried red chillies

sea salt

6 sprigs of fresh thyme

1 sprig of fresh rosemary, broken into pieces

6 fresh bay leaves

1 celery heart

2 carrots, peeled

1 red onion, peeled

4 garlic cloves, peeled and cut in half

For the sauce

extra virgin olive oil

4 tablespoons plain flour, for dusting

1 x 400g tin of peeled plum tomatoes

sea salt and freshly ground black pepper

100ml double cream

80g Parmesan, freshly grated, plus extra for serving

500g fresh or dried pappardelle

Cut the hare into pieces: divide the saddle on the bone into 4, and cut the hind and front legs off the carcass. Put all the pieces into a large bowl. Add the wine, spices, chillies, salt and fresh herbs. Cut the celery into 2cm chunks, and do the same with the carrots and the onion. Add the vegetables and garlic to the marinade, pushing everything down into the wine and making sure the hare is covered. Cover the bowl and leave to marinate in a cool place or in the fridge for at least 24 hours.

Choose a large, thick-bottomed pan into which all the pieces of hare will fit in one layer. Take the pieces of hare out of the marinade, pat dry with kitchen paper, and dust with flour. Drain the vegetables, spices and herbs and put into a bowl, separating out the spices from the vegetables and reserving the liquid marinade separately.

Heat 4 tablespoons of olive oil in the large pan. When hot, add the floured hare pieces and let them brown on all sides. Remove to a metal bowl and keep in a warm place. Now add the drained vegetables and herbs to the pan – you may have to add a little more olive oil – and let them brown for 10 minutes, or until they have begun to soften. Return the hare pieces and any extra juices in the bowl to the pan and pour over the reserved marinade. Now add the spices from the marinade, plus the plum tomatoes, and bring to the boil. Season with sea salt, turn the heat down and simmer gently for 1 hour. Add a little hot water if the sauce is drying up. Turn the hare pieces over, cover, and continue to cook for a further 30 minutes or until the meat is falling off the bone. Remove from the heat and leave until cool enough to be able to pick the meat from the bones. Discard the cinnamon, juniper, peppercorns, thyme and rosemary. Put the meat and vegetables into a food processor with the remaining juices and pulse-chop until you have a thick sauce.

Pour the sauce into a pan, add the cream, and bring to boiling point. Cook for 2–3 minutes, stirring in the Parmesan and checking for seasoning.

Cook the pappardelle in boiling salted water until al dente. Drain, keeping back a little of the cooking water, and add to the sauce, tossing the pappardelle to coat each ribbon. Add a little of the cooking water if the sauce is too thick. Serve on warm plates, with extra Parmesan on the side.

Making ravioli for the August ravioli festival in Contignano

RAVIOLI CON RICOTTA

RAVIOLI STUFFED WITH RICOTTA

Creamy fresh ricotta is made by most cheesemakers. In Italy the most delicate and delicious ricotta is made with sheep's milk and buffalo milk, a by-product of Pecorino and mozzarella. This fresh cheese is made by re-cooking the whey that is part of the initial process of the making of the full-fat cheese – hence the word 'ricotta'.

We were in the Maremma one year visiting a Pecorino producer and the enthusiastic cheesemakers insisted we tried the ricotta curds warm as they were forming in the whey. The taste lives with us for ever: sweet and overpowering.

In Calabria, buffalo ricotta is used to stuff these ravioli. The texture is very fine and creamy and the cooks there like to keep the ravioli quite plain, using a rich nutty sauce to go with them. The walnuts come from Sorrento, which is one of the areas of Italy famous for their cultivation.

For 12

1 x quantity of fresh pasta dough (see page 40)

500g fresh buffalo or sheep's ricotta

sea salt and freshly ground black pepper

3 tablespoons very finely chopped fresh flat-leaf parsley, plus extra for serving

100g flour, for dusting

3 tablespoons extra virgin olive oil

50g Parmesan, freshly grated

For the sauce

400g wet walnuts in their shells (150g shelled weight)

½ a ciabatta loaf, crusts removed

350ml milk

1 garlic clove, peeled

½ a nutmeg, grated

sea salt and freshly ground black pepper

250g fresh buffalo or sheep's ricotta

Make the fresh pasta, wrap in clingfilm and refrigerate for 1 hour.

To make the sauce, shell the walnuts, then peel off the bitter skin. This is made easier by pouring boiling water over the nuts and leaving them to cool in the water. Soak the bread in the milk for 5 minutes or until it is soft, then break it up.

Put the walnuts into a food processor with the garlic, soaked bread and enough of the milk to blend into a creamy sauce. Add the nutmeg and seasoning.

Beat the ricotta lightly with a fork, then fold in the walnut mixture and half the Parmesan. If the sauce is too thick, dilute it with some more of the milk – the consistency should be like double cream.

Now assemble the ravioli. Beat the ricotta, season it, and mix in half the parsley. Now divide your pasta dough into 4 balls and roll out on the finest setting of your pasta machine to get thin sheets. Place 1 teaspoon of the ricotta mixture on the dough at 4cm intervals along the length and spray with a fine mist of water before folding the dough over to cover the ricotta spoonfuls. Press gently with your finger to seal the dough together, then cut into ravioli, either with a zigzag cutter or with a knife on three sides, the fourth side being the folded one. Place the ravioli on a floured tray while you finish making them.

Bring a large pan of salted water to the boil and drop in the ravioli in batches. Remove with a slotted spoon after 3 minutes; they will rise to the surface when nearly cooked, but give them an extra minute to make sure the pasta is cooked around the edges where it is thickest. Use a warm bowl drizzled with extra virgin olive oil to serve your ravioli.

Gently heat the sauce while the ravioli are cooking; do not boil.

Serve the ravioli on warm plates. Spoon a little of the sauce on to each plate, then place the ravioli over the sauce and add a further spoonful of sauce on top. Sprinkle with the rest of the parsley and the remaining Parmesan.

SPAGHETTI ALLE VONGOLE CON BURRO

SPAGHETTI WITH CLAMS AND BUTTER

Using butter is an unusual choice for cooking clams, as most recipes call for olive oil. This recipe comes from a restaurant called Puntarossa Da Renatone on the beach near Fumancino, close to Rome. The butter emulsifies with the wine, making the sauce deliciously creamy.

For 6
75g butter
extra virgin olive oil
2 garlic cloves, peeled and chopped
1 dried red chilli, crushed
sea salt and freshly ground black pepper
1kg small clams, washed
½ bunch of fresh flat-leaf parsley, leaves picked and chopped
250ml Vermentino wine
400g dried spaghetti

Check over the clams and discard any that are not closed. Place half the butter in a wide pan with 2 tablespoons of olive oil, the garlic and chilli. Season with sea salt and freshly ground black pepper. Fry for a minute, then add the clams and parsley and toss over the heat. Add the wine and cover with a lid. Cook for about 5 minutes, depending on the size of the pan and the clams, shaking the pan from time to time.

In the meantime, cook the spaghetti in plenty of boiling salted water until al dente. When the clams are open (discard any that remain closed), mix them with the drained spaghetti and toss with the remaining butter.

For an alternative that is equally delicious, prepare the clams as above, but omit the butter. When the clams are cooked, place them in a bowl around the circumference of which are oven-toasted crostini rubbed with garlic, placed so that they sit halfway into the broth.

SPAGHETTI CON BOTTARGA

SPAGHETTI WITH DRIED GREY MULLET ROE

We are always learning from friends the subtle differences in their favourite recipes. Bottarga, the delicious sun-dried grey mullet roe, is an ingredient primarily found in the cooking of Sardinia, shaved over salads, or finely grated and melted into olive oil as a sauce for spaghetti. This summer in Tuscany we were served a wonderful plate of pasta that combined bottarga and fresh cherry tomatoes, which was both spicy and sweet. It was that family's pasta dish and an exciting new recipe to try out when we returned to the River Café.

For 4

250g ripe soft cherry tomatoes

2 garlic cloves, peeled and sliced

2 tablespoons chopped fresh flat-leaf parsley

2 dried red chillies, crumbled

freshly ground black pepper

extra virgin olive oil

150g bottarga di muggine

350g spaghetti

sea salt

Tear the cherry tomatoes into small pieces, squeezing out the seeds, and put into a bowl. Finely chop the garlic with the parsley and add to the tomatoes. Season with the chilli and pepper only, pour in 3 tablespoons of olive oil and stir to combine. Set aside for 30 minutes to let the flavours develop. Meanwhile grate the bottarga on the finest side of a cheese grater, reserving a little to grate over the finished dish.

Bring a large pan of salted water to the boil, add the spaghetti and, while the pasta is cooking, heat the tomatoes in a separate pan. When the spaghetti is al dente, drain it and return it to the saucepan. Add the bottarga and 2 tablespoons of olive oil and toss, making sure to coat each strand, then stir in the tomatoes. If the sauce is too thick, add a further drizzle of olive oil. Test for seasoning and serve with a little bottarga freshly grated over each plate.

Bottarga, the delicious sun-dried grey mullet roe, is an ingredient primarily found in the cooking of Sardinia, shaved over salads, or finely grated and melted into olive oil as a sauce for spaghetti

SPAGHETTI ALLA PUTTANESCA

The ingredients in this pasta sauce remind us of Italy's wonderful street markets, particularly in the south – the array of tomatoes alongside the specialist stalls that display salted anchovies packed tightly in 5kg tins, the mounds of capers preserved in sea salt, and the delicious selection of local olives.

For 6

extra virgin olive oil

4 garlic cloves, peeled and finely sliced

6 anchovy fillets, roughly chopped

2 tablespoons dried oregano

2 dried red chillies, crumbled

3 tablespoons salted capers, rinsed in a sieve under a cold running tap, chopped

4 tablespoons small black olives, stoned and torn in half

5 tablespoons finely chopped fresh flat-leaf parsley

750g ripe plum tomatoes, peeled, cored and finely chopped

sea salt and freshly ground black pepper

500g spaghetti

1 lemon

Heat 3 tablespoons of olive oil in a wide, thick-bottomed pan. Add the garlic and reduce the heat. When the garlic begins to brown, add the anchovies, oregano and chilli, stirring them into the oil. Cook briefly, just to melt the anchovies.

Add half the capers, half the olives and half the parsley, stir well to combine, then add the tomatoes. Bring the sauce to the boil, then reduce the heat and simmer until the tomatoes become thick, stirring from time to time to prevent sticking. This should take about 20–30 minutes. Season with sea salt and black pepper.

Bring a large pan of salted water to the boil. Add the spaghetti and cook until al dente. Drain and add to the sauce, then stir in the remaining olives, capers and parsley. Finish with a drizzle of extra virgin olive oil and a squeeze of lemon.

PICI AL LIMONE CON PECORINO

PICI WITH LEMON AND PECORINO SAUCE

Pici is a handmade pasta made with plain flour and water which is only found in Tuscany, in the area south of Siena. A sauce of lemon juice, olive oil, freshly grated Pecorino cheese, possibly a few leaves of fresh basil, goes perfectly with a hard wheat string pasta such as spaghetti, linguine or bucatini (if you can't find pici). Versions of this sauce can be found from Tuscany to Naples.

Staying near Pienza this summer, and having purchased a packet of dried locally made pici, we decided to make this sauce using both fresh and aged Pecorino made close by, with lemons and basil from the garden. The only ingredient that had travelled more than ten kilometres was the olive oil, which had been made in Felsina in Castelnuovo Baradenga, the other side of Siena, thirty-five kilometres away.

For 4

325g pici or bucatini, i.e. thick spaghetti

sea salt and freshly ground black pepper

2–3 lemons

350g fresh Pecorino

50g Pecorino staginato (aged)

4 tablespoons extra virgin olive oil

a bunch of fresh basil, leaves picked

Pici takes about 10 minutes to cook, in which time you can make the sauce. Cook the pici in a large pan of boiling salted water until al dente. Squeeze the lemons – you need about 150ml of juice. Grate the fresh Pecorino on the coarser side of the grater. Grate the aged Pecorino. Place the lemon juice in a bowl and add the fresh cheese, stirring it into the mixture; the cheese should melt into the juice. Add the olive oil slowly until it has combined, making a thick lumpy sauce. Put the sauce into a warm pan.

Drain the pasta, keeping back a little of the cooking water. Put the drained pici back into the pan you cooked them in and add 2 tablespoons of the hot cooking water. Add the sauce and basil leaves and toss until all the pici strands are coated. Finally, stir in half the grated aged Pecorino. Serve the remaining aged cheese on the side.

Fresh lemon sauce
simply made without
any cooking makes a
favourite summer pasta

PENNE CON STRACOTTO

PENNE WITH BEEF BRAISED IN CHIANTI

When beef is marinated for 24 hours and then cooked for 3 to 4 hours, it becomes soft and buttery. It breaks easily with a fork into a sauce that is ideal for a hard pasta like penne. This recipe was cooked for us by our Florentine friend Lucia Bartolini. She used the Italian cut of meat called sorra di manzo, which is chuck steak in the UK. It's cut from near the shoulder and should have good marbling and a loose texture.

For 6

500g beef chuck steak, or other stewing beef

1 bottle Chianti Classico

sea salt and freshly ground black pepper

extra virgin olive oil

1 small head of celery, white parts only

1 small red onion, peeled

3 garlic cloves, peeled

a small bunch of fresh sage, leaves picked

2 sprigs of fresh rosemary, leaves picked

5 juniper berries

4 cloves

10g dried porcini (soaked for 30 minutes in 300ml hot water)

20g pine nuts

4 bay leaves, fresh if possible

1 lemon, zested

500g penne

100g Parmesan, freshly grated

Put the meat into a bowl and add enough wine to cover. Leave to marinate at room temperature for 24 hours.

When you are ready to cook, remove the meat from the marinade and dry with kitchen paper, reserving the marinade. Season with plenty of salt. Heat 2 tablespoons of extra virgin olive oil in a thick-bottomed pan and brown the meat well.

Roughly chop together the celery, onion, garlic, sage, rosemary, juniper and cloves. Drain the porcini, pat dry with kitchen paper, roughly chop and add to the mixture. Add this mixture to the beef, stir to combine, and add the pine nuts and bay leaves. Season with black pepper and cook for 5 minutes. Add the marinade, raise the heat until the liquid comes to the boil, then lower to a simmer and cover.

Cook for 3–4 hours, adding the strained porcini liquid and more wine if needed. There should always be enough liquid to keep the meat moist. The meat should be extremely tender, able to be cut with a fork.

When the meat is done, remove from the pan and roughly chop. Return to the pan with the lemon zest and enough oil to make it very wet.

Cook the penne in a large pan of boiling salted water until al dente. Drain, reserving a little of the cooking water, and stir the sauce through the pasta, adding some of the cooking water if too thick. Serve with Parmesan scattered over.

Penne with beef braised in Chianti

BUCATINI CON ACCIUGHE

BUCATINI WITH SALTED ANCHOVIES

This recipe comes from a trattoria in the hilltop village of Dogliani in Piedmont, where there is a wonderful street food market. One of the stalls sells only salted and smoked fish, including many grades of salted anchovies for every kind of use, as well as a wide selection of stockafissa, baccalà and salted sardines. In particular, it has the rare large red Spanish anchovies that are fished from the Cantabrian Sea near San Sebastián. They are packed whole into 10kg tins and have the most delicious, delicate flavour.

It is very sad that Cantabrian anchovies have been overfished and very few are now available in tins for us to buy. The Mediterranean anchovy is the alternative; it is a smaller fish, which means it is more salty, but it also has a good flavour.

This pasta sauce relies on the flavour of the anchovies, so try to source the real salted anchovies sold out of 5kg or 10kg tins from an Italian, Spanish or Greek delicatessen. Avoid the little jars, as these anchovies are usually too small and the flavour is not strong enough for this dish.

For 4

4 tablespoons extra virgin olive oil

2 garlic cloves, peeled and finely chopped

12 salted anchovy fillets, washed and roughly chopped

2 dried red chillies, crumbled

freshly ground black pepper

1 lemon, zested and juiced

3 tablespoons finely chopped fresh flat-leaf parsley

350g bucatini or pici

For the pangrattato

100ml extra virgin olive oil

4 garlic cloves, peeled but left whole

1 small ciabatta loaf, crusts removed, pulsed into coarse breadcrumbs

First make the pangrattato. Heat the oil in a small pan, add the whole garlic cloves and cook gently over a low heat for about 5 minutes, until brown. Remove the garlic from the oil and discard. Add the breadcrumbs to the pan, push them down into the hot oil and cook for about 5–10 minutes, until crisp and golden. Drain on kitchen paper.

To make the sauce, heat the oil in a medium thick-bottomed pan. Add the chopped garlic and fry for about 2 minutes, until it begins to colour, then reduce the heat and add the anchovies. Break them up with a wooden spoon so that they combine with the garlic. This must be done over a low heat, as you don't want to fry the anchovies, just melt them. After about 5 minutes, crumble in the chillies and season with black pepper. Remove from the heat, add the lemon zest and juice and the parsley. Taste – if the flavour is too strong, add a little extra virgin olive oil.

Cook the bucatini in boiling salted water until al dente. Drain, keeping back a little of the pasta cooking water. Add the sauce to the bucatini with 3 tablespoons of the water and toss over a low heat for 2–3 minutes, to coat each strand. Finally, mix in the pangrattato. Serve in warmed bowls.

FUSILLI CON ZUCCHINI

FUSILLI WITH ZUCCHINI AND BUTTER

In 1986, the summer before we opened the River Café, we stayed in a house on the Amalfi coast. On the way back to Naples we made a detour to Marina del Cantone, a small seaside town not far from Positano, where we had been told there was a trattoria called Lo Scoglio where they made the best fusilli with zucchini.

This recipe is the closest to it, sweet and buttery – a perfect pasta to make in the heat of summer.

For 4
250g zucchini
1 tablespoon extra virgin olive oil
1 garlic clove, peeled and cut into slivers
150g butter, softened
320g fusilli
50g Parmesan, grated

Wash the zucchini, dry them, and trim the ends. Cut them into 1cm thick discs.

Heat the olive oil in a frying pan large enough to hold the zucchini in one layer. Add the garlic to the oil and then, once soft, add the zucchini. Season and stir until just beginning to brown. Add half the butter, stir and lower the heat. Continue cooking, adding a small amount of water to loosen the bits stuck to the pan. Stir and scrape until the zucchini have become soft and creamy. Remove from the heat and stir in the remaining butter.

Cook the fusilli in boiling salted water, according to the packet instructions, until al dente. Drain, reserving a little of the cooking water. Stir this into the zucchini to loosen the sauce.

Add the fusilli to the sauce and toss very well. Serve with the grated Parmesan.

PENNE ALL' ARRABBIATA

PENNE WITH TOMATO AND CHILLI SAUCE

In Italy many cooks grow their own chillies. They grow easily in pots and need only sunshine and minimal water to flourish. Harvested chilli plants are tied together and hung upside down to dry in the autumn. You can buy these in the markets, and one bunch should keep you going until the following year. Near Lucca, in Bar Pieve, in Pieve di Camione, we ate penne all' arrabbiata at least once a week during the summer. They always used their own home-grown chillies, garlic and tomatoes. The chillies were dried and strong, the garlic cloves were small and sweet, and the tomatoes had a wonderful flavour. To re-create the sauce we used tinned tomatoes. In Lucca, where we have often eaten penne all' arrabbiata, they never serve cheese of any kind with this dish.

Tinned tomatoes vary hugely. As a starting point, buy peeled plum tomatoes tinned in their own juice, not those in pulp, which could be made from other varieties of tomatoes. Buy tomatoes that are grown in Campagna and Puglia, as the tomatoes are grown outside, ripen in the sun, and have a full flavour. San Marzano is the best variety for sauce.

For 4–5
extra virgin olive oil
4 garlic cloves, peeled and cut in half if large, or kept whole
4 whole large dried red chillies
2 x 400g tins of Italian plum tomatoes
sea salt and freshly ground black pepper
350g penne
extra virgin olive oil
a small bunch of fresh basil, leaves picked

Heat 3 tablespoons of extra virgin olive oil in a thick-bottomed pan over a medium heat. Add the garlic cloves, let them lightly brown, then add the whole chillies and stir just to coat them with the oil. Add the tomatoes and their juice and 1 teaspoon of sea salt, bring to the boil, then reduce the heat and cook, stirring from time to time and breaking up the chillies and tomatoes, until you have a thick sauce; this will take 30 minutes or more. Add black pepper to taste.

Cook the penne in boiling salted water until al dente, drain and return to the pan. Generously drizzle over some strong-flavoured extra virgin olive oil and add the basil. Finally add the sauce and, keeping the saucepan on a low heat, stir and toss until every piece of penne is evenly coated with tomato. Serve in hot bowls.

SPAGHETTI ALLA CARBONARA

There are many versions of this classic recipe. This one was inspired by the version we ate in the restaurant Carbonni, in the Piazza Campo dei Fiori in Rome.

For 6

150g pancetta, sliced 3mm thick

1 tablespoon extra virgin olive oil

1 red onion, peeled and finely chopped

400g dried spaghetti

3 tablespoons fresh flat-leaf parsley, chopped

30g unsalted butter, softened

50g Pecorino, freshly grated

50g Parmesan, freshly grated

9 large free-range organic egg yolks

Cut the pancetta into matchsticks. Heat the olive oil in a thick-bottomed pan and fry the onion for about 15 minutes, until very soft and translucent but not brown. Lower the heat as much as possible and add the pancetta. Cook until brown, but not crisp – about 10 minutes. Keep warm on a low heat.

Meanwhile, cook the spaghetti in boiling salted water until al dente and drain.

Still over a low heat, add the parsley and butter to the pancetta. When the butter is melted and the pan is hot, add the spaghetti and toss well to coat each strand. Add the Pecorino and half the Parmesan, then immediately add the egg yolks. Toss well, but be careful not to let the pan get too hot – the eggs must not scramble but must coat the pasta to form a creamy sauce. Serve with the remaining Parmesan sprinkled over.

SMOOTH PENNE WITH FRIED AUBERGINE AND SALTED RICOTTA

Salted ricotta is made in the south of Italy. The fresh strained curds are placed in brine for a few days, then air-dried to develop into a hard grating cheese that keeps indefinitely. Its salty taste is used by cooks to complement sweet tomatoes that are made into sauces for pasta every day.

For 4
1 pale, round aubergine
sea salt and freshly ground black pepper
8 ripe plum tomatoes
2 garlic cloves, peeled
a bunch of fresh basil, leaves picked
500ml sunflower oil
2 tablespoons red wine vinegar
230g penne lisce
80g ricotta salata (a hard, aged ricotta suitable for grating)

Cut the aubergine into fine slices no more than 5mm thick. Place on kitchen paper and sprinkle with sea salt. Leave for at least 30 minutes, then rinse each slice under cold water and pat dry.

To peel the tomatoes, score down one side, place in a large bowl, and pour over boiling water to cover. Remove them immediately to another large bowl, filled with cold water, and slip off the skins the moment the tomatoes are cool enough to handle. Place them on a chopping board, cut each tomato in half lengthwise, then chop the halves roughly. Keeping all the juices, scrape up and place in a bowl. Season with sea salt.

Finely chop the garlic, then add ½ teaspoon of salt. Grind the garlic with the salt using the end of a knife, flat side down on the board, to make a paste. Stir this paste into the tomatoes. Tear up half the basil leaves and add to the tomatoes.

Heat the sunflower oil in a large thick-bottomed, low-sided, flat pan. Test for the correct temperature, 120°C, by putting in a slice of aubergine; it should turn a light golden colour almost immediately. Remove with a slotted spoon on to kitchen paper. Repeat the process with the rest of the aubergines, frying only one layer at a time. Sprinkle the fried aubergine with the vinegar.

Bring a large pan of salted water to the boil. Add the penne and cook according to the packet instructions until al dente. While the penne is cooking, put the tomato mixture into a large pan and heat gently until hot, but not cooked. Grate the ricotta.

Drain the penne and add to the tomato mixture, stirring to coat each piece of pasta with the sauce. Gently fold in the aubergine slices, season, and add the remaining basil. Spoon the pasta into warm bowls and scatter the grated ricotta over each serving.

Palazzo della Torre, Verona

RISOTTO & POLENTA

RISOTTO & POLENTA

The twenty minutes it takes to transform rice and a few seasonal ingredients into a luscious risotto is, for us, one of the most enjoyable and satisfying cooking experiences. A regional dish found only in northern Italy, risotto is made with varieties of rice, uniquely Italian, grown alongside the great river Po. The river starts its course in the lower slopes of the Maritime Alps, where the rice fields are fed by water from the melting snow, and continues its journey to the Adriatic Sea.

There are three different varieties of risotto rice available to choose from: Arborio, Vialone Nano and Carnaroli. They all have a soft starch on the outside of the grain which slowly dissolves during cooking, absorbing the flavour of the liquid added, and a tougher starch in the centre which stays firm and gives the rice its bite.

Arborio is a large plump grain that has a high amount of soft starch. The Milanese love cooking with this, and use it for the famous risotto alla Milanese, but it does require constant attention to achieve the perfect consistency.

Vialone Nano is a smaller-grained variety with a thick coat of slightly tougher starch that breaks down slowly into a creamy, binding liquid – an important element of a risotto. Venetians favour this variety for their fish risottos, usually made with wine, producing a soupier texture but with the kernel retaining a firm bite.

Our favourite rice for risotto is the Carnaroli variety. It was developed by an Italian rice grower just after the war by crossing the Arborio strain with a Japanese variety. Carnaroli is a plump grain sheathed in the important soft starch, which dissolves deliciously when cooked, but it also has a larger proportion of the inner tough starch, which helps keep the rice both firm and moist and easier for the cook to manage.

There are three stages in cooking a risotto. The first is the soffrito base, and this will vary depending on which risotto you are making. It is usually made just from onion, sometimes onion, celery and garlic, or, in some fish risottos, just garlic cooked in butter and/or olive oil. The soffrito must cook sufficiently for the flavours to blend into the soft starch of the rice.

The second stage begins when you increase the heat and stir in the unwashed rice to the soffrito until each grain is coated and becomes opaque. This stage is quickly followed by the third, the adding of the stock. To make a successful risotto, the stock should be gently simmering and well seasoned, and then added gradually so that the rice can absorb the flavour. Use a wooden spoon to stir the risotto around and scrape the sides and bottom of the pan, but don't let the liquid evaporate too quickly. When all the liquid is absorbed, then, and only then, add the next ladleful of stock. It is important to stir all the time when making a risotto, so that every grain of rice absorbs the liquid at the same rate. Near the end of cooking, add the stock in half ladles so that the rice remains moist and creamy – by doing this you can keep control and avoid overcooking it.

Finally, we stir cheese and butter into some risottos, herbs or blanched vegetables or extra virgin olive oil into others. Whatever you add, stir it in well so that it blends totally into the rice, and serve at once on hot plates.

RISOTTO CON LATTE

RISOTTO WITH MILK

The Bar Giocosa in the Via Tornabuoni in Florence was a very chic place and held a fascination for us. It's probably because of the diversity of what they offered in that tiny space: the deliciousness of the pasta, panini, pizzette and risotti, the variety of drinks, including an extraordinary array of amari and every style of spumante and prosecco. There, at any time of day, we would watch an array of elegant characters at the bar eating little plates of risotto con latte, some accompanied by a glass of prosecco.

For 6

500ml chicken stock

sea salt and freshly ground black pepper

1 litre milk

1 celery heart, white part only, finely chopped

1 white onion, peeled and finely chopped

120g unsalted butter

300g Carnaroli risotto rice

½ a nutmeg, grated

60g Parmesan, freshly grated

3 tablespoons double cream

6 slices prosciutto crudo (optional)

Bring the chicken stock to a gentle simmer and check for seasoning. Heat the milk separately and keep warm. Slowly melt half the butter in a medium thick-bottomed pan. Add the celery and onion and cook very gently until soft. This will take about 5–6 minutes.

Turn up the heat a little and add the rice, stirring it into the mixture to coat each grain. Cook for 2 minutes, until the rice becomes opaque, then add the nutmeg. Add the stock, one ladleful at a time, stirring to prevent the rice from sticking, and adding more stock only when the previous ladleful has been absorbed. When the stock is used up, start adding the warm milk. Cook, stirring occasionally, for about 15 minutes, or until the rice is al dente.

Remove from the heat and add the remaining butter and the Parmesan. Let the butter melt into the rice for a minute, then check the seasoning. Just before serving, add the cream, stir very briefly, and serve on warm plates with a slice of prosciutto crudo.

RISOTTO CON BRUSCANDOLI

RISOTTO WITH WILD HOP SHOOTS

In April the grand VinItaly wine fair takes place in Verona. We always go, as it offers a chance to meet Italian winemakers from every region, to taste the new vintages, to be introduced to new wines and, equally important, to go out to eat with all who are caught up in this fabulous festival. Enoteca della Valpolicella is a favourite restaurant not just for its food and incredible wine but also for this delicious and unique risotto, made with locally picked bruscandoli. They look a bit like sprue asparagus, which you can also use for this recipe, only the stems are very thin and slightly hairy and the leaves and tips of the shoots are purplish green. The flavour is somewhere between asparagus and nettles, a slightly earthy bitter taste which is complemented with lots of Italian unsalted butter and aged Parmesan or Grano Padano, which is a cheese made in the region of Parma.

For 4

500g bruscandoli (wild hop shoots), washed

1.5 litres chicken stock

sea salt and freshly ground black pepper

125g unsalted butter

1 large red onion, peeled and finely chopped

350g Carnaroli risotto rice

100ml Soave Classico

50g Grano Padano or Parmesan, grated

Cut the tips and leaves off the bruscandoli. Place the stalks on a board and chop them finely as you would parsley. Keep the leaves and tips to one side.

Bring the stock to a gentle simmer. Test for seasoning. Melt half the butter in a thick-bottomed pan over a medium heat, add the onion and cook gently for about 10 minutes until completely soft. Add the bruscandoli stalks to the onion and cook together for 2–3 minutes. Add the rice and stir to make sure each grain is coated well. Cook until the rice is opaque, which will take 3 or 4 minutes, then add the wine. Stir, scraping up any grains that may have stuck together, until the wine is absorbed. Then start to add the stock, a ladleful at a time, only adding more when the previous stock has been absorbed.

After ten minutes of cooking add the bruscandoli leaves and tips and continue stirring, adding the stock until the rice is al dente. Remove the risotto from the heat, beat in the remaining butter and finally stir in the Grano Padano or Parmesan.

RISOTTO ALLA MILANESE

The golden colour of this gleaming risotto comes from the prized spice saffron, still one of the most expensive and cared-for ingredients in northern Italy. Ossobuco di vitello is the dish that is traditionally served in Milan with saffron risotto.

For 6

1.5 litres veal stock

4 pieces of veal shin bone, sawn off to expose the marrow

sea salt and freshly ground white pepper

125g unsalted butter

1 large white or red sweet onion, peeled and finely chopped

350g Carnaroli risotto rice

100ml dry white vermouth

1 teaspoon saffron threads, dissolved in 125ml hot stock

80g Parmesan, freshly grated

Bring the stock up to a light simmer in a large thick-bottomed saucepan. Add the veal bones and keep simmering. Check the seasoning.

Melt half the butter in a high-sided thick-bottomed pan and add the onion. Turn down the heat and cook slowly for about 10 minutes, until the onion is soft and translucent. Add the rice and stir for a few minutes to coat each grain with the butter, until the rice glistens and becomes opaque. Pour in the vermouth and let it bubble and become absorbed, then start to add the stock a ladleful at a time, stirring to make sure the rice is not sticking to the pan and is cooking evenly. As soon as the stock has been absorbed by the rice, add a further ladleful, adding the saffron and its liquid at this stage, and continue to add stock in this way until the rice is al dente.

Take the risotto off the heat and stir in the remaining butter and half the Parmesan.

Take the veal bones from the stock and on a board knock them hard so that the marrowbone jelly falls out. Serve the risotto on warm plates, with a generous spoonful of the marrowbone jelly on top and the rest of the Parmesan on the side.

RISOTTO CON PESCHE

WHITE PEACH RISOTTO WITH PROSECCO

We make this risotto in the summer, when the white peaches are ripe and juicy. It is the only fruit risotto we know. Choose a sweet spring onion, or a mild-flavoured white one, so as not to overpower the delicacy of the peaches.

For 6

350g whole ripe white peaches

½ a bottle of prosecco

1 lemon

80g butter

1 medium white onion, peeled and finely chopped

350g Carnaroli risotto rice

1.5 litres chicken or vegetable stock

a small bunch of fresh basil, leaves picked

50g Parmesan, grated, plus extra for serving

sea salt and freshly ground black pepper

Drop the peaches into boiling water for 10 seconds. Remove from the water, peel off the skins, cut in half and remove the stones. Cut into small pieces and put into a bowl. Pour over half the prosecco and add a small squeeze of lemon juice. Cover with clingfilm and leave to marinate for half an hour, then smash the peaches to a coarse pulp with a fork.

In a thick-bottomed pan gently heat 60g of the butter. Add the onion and cook on a low heat for about 10 minutes, until soft and translucent but not browned. Add the rice and stir to coat each grain with the butter. Add the second half of the prosecco and cook until the wine has evaporated. Begin to add the stock, one ladleful at a time, and continue until the rice is almost cooked, stirring often. Stir in the peaches and cook till the rice becomes al dente. Stir through the remaining butter and the Parmesan, tear in the basil leaves, season to taste and serve, with extra Parmesan alongside.

RISOTTO CON VONGOLE

FENNEL AND CLAM RISOTTO

Adding vegetables to our fish risottos gives an extra dimension. In the summer we might cook peas or tomatoes with clams, in the winter we might use fennel. Put the fennel in at the beginning; the long slow cooking allows the sweet flavour to permeate the risotto, contrasting with the saltiness of the clams.

For 6
For the clams
2 tablespoons extra virgin olive oil
2 garlic cloves, peeled and chopped
1.5kg clams, washed
50ml Pinot Bianco, or other dry white wine

For the risotto
1.5 litres fish stock
25g butter
1 garlic clove, peeled and finely chopped
1 small fennel bulb, chopped, leafy tops reserved
350g Carnaroli risotto rice
150ml Pinot Bianco, as above
30g cold butter, chopped

Check over the clams and discard any that are not closed. Heat the olive oil in a pan large enough to hold the clams. Add the garlic and cook gently for about 5 minutes, until just soft. Add the clams and stir to coat with the oil and garlic, then add the wine. Cover the pan and cook until the clams are open (discard any that remain closed). When cool remove them from their shells. Sieve the liquid into a bowl and add the clams, to keep them moist.

Heat the fish stock and leave over a low heat. Melt the 25g of butter in a thick-bottomed pan. Add the garlic and chopped fennel. Cook for 5 minutes, then add the rice and stir to coat each grain with the butter. Add the wine, stir, and allow to evaporate. Add the stock one ladleful at a time, only adding more when the previous ladleful has been absorbed.

Continue adding stock until the rice is al dente. During the last minutes add the clams and their juices. Remove the pan from the heat and stir in the fennel tops and the cold butter.

RISOTTO NERO

CUTTLEFISH RISOTTO

Last summer in Venice we explored the dark secrets of risotto nero. In just one week in various bars and restaurants we ate seven, and all were different. Some were made only with the ink from the fish, some were quite pale, made only with fish stock. The best was a risotto that was creamy and wet, with plenty of soft buttery cuttlefish nestling among the rice grains, the liquid not too dense, with a hint of tomato and wine and a touch of chilli.

For 6

1.5 litres fish stock or water

sea salt and freshly ground black pepper

3 tablespoons extra virgin olive oil

1 red onion or sweet white onion, peeled and finely chopped

2 garlic cloves, peeled and chopped

1kg cuttlefish or squid (only very small ones are suitable), cleaned and roughly chopped; keep any ink sacs you find

1 dried red chilli, crumbled

350g Vialone Nano risotto rice

125ml white wine (choose a northern Italian wine such as Soave Classico, made in the same region that the dish originates from)

4 plum tomatoes (either fresh ones, skinned, or from a tin, chopped)

2 sachets of cuttlefish ink

3 tablespoons chopped fresh flat-leaf parsley

If using fish stock, bring it to simmering point in a pan and check the seasoning.

To make the risotto, choose a thick-bottomed pan with sides at least as high as the width of the pan. This proportion helps keep the liquid in your risotto from evaporating too quickly when stirring it into the rice, giving the rice a chance to expand and absorb the flavour gently.

Pour in the olive oil and add the onion. Cook over a medium heat for about 10 minutes, until the onion has softened and is beginning to colour. Add the garlic and cook for a minute or two, then add the cuttlefish pieces – not the ink at this stage – and the chilli, and season. Stir to combine, then add the rice and stir so that it is well mixed in; this should take only 2–3 minutes. When the rice becomes opaque, add the wine and tomatoes and cook until the rice has absorbed the liquid. Stir to prevent sticking.

At this point add the ink from the sachets, plus any ink sacs you have reserved, and then, when each grain of rice has become black, start to add the stock, a ladleful at a time, stirring to make sure the rice is separated from the sides and bottom of the pan. Continue to add stock, only when the previous ladleful has been absorbed, until the rice is cooked al dente, firm with a little bite.

Remove from the heat and stir in the parsley. Check for seasoning and serve. Some people add a little butter at this point, but if you have plenty of the rich, creamy ink, butter is not necessary.

Riseria Gazzani, Verona

RISOTTO CON PISELLI

RISOTTO WITH PEAS AND PROSCIUTTO

In Venice in the spring you will find peas included in nearly every dish. The vegetable stalls there sell peas on the vine, with their leaves attached, to be used in stocks and soups. They also sell peas already podded and graded into sizes, for busy Venetian cooks. The peas at this time of the year are so sweet and juicy, perfect for the following recipe. There is a legendary motto for this risotto: 'A pea for every grain of rice.'

For 6

1.5 litres chicken stock
2kg small fresh peas, podded (keep half the pods and wash them)
sea salt and freshly ground black pepper
6 slices prosciutto di San Daniele, with plenty of fat
120g unsalted butter
3 red spring onions the size of golf balls, or equivalent, peeled and finely chopped
2 tablespoons finely chopped fresh flat-leaf parsley
350g Carnaroli risotto rice
70g Parmesan, grated

Bring the stock to the boil in a large pan and add the pea pods. Simmer gently for about 20 minutes, until soft, then drain into a second pan. Purée the pods, and stir this purée back into the stock. Check the seasoning.

Finely chop the prosciutto, including its fat. Heat 3 tablespoons of butter in a thick-bottomed pan over a medium heat. Add the prosciutto and cook until the fat runs, then add the onions. Turn the heat down and cook for about 5 minutes, until the onions are soft. Add the peas and 1 tablespoon of parsley and cook just long enough to coat the peas, then add the rice and stir to combine the prosciutto, peas and rice. The rice should glisten and become opaque. At this point, add the stock a ladleful at a time, stirring to prevent the rice from sticking. As soon as the stock has been absorbed by the rice, add a further ladleful. Continue this process until the rice is al dente.

Finally, stir in the remaining parsley, the Parmesan and the rest of the butter and remove from the heat. Serve on warm plates.

RISOTTO AL BAROLO

RISOTTO WITH BAROLO

Barolo wine is made in and around the commune of Barolo in Piedmont. This wonderful, powerful wine is made from Nebbiolo grapes, the character of which is intense, with fruity, delicate perfumes and subtle oak flavours. When making this risotto, the idea is to keep these intense flavours and not to overpower them with either the stock or the Parmesan. So it is very important to test the stock you use for seasoning and flavour, and to dilute it if it seems too strong. Adding the cheese at the end should be done with caution. We add the last third of the bottle of Barolo at the end of cooking, just so that the colour and flavour is as bright as the wine itself.

For 6

1 bottle of Barolo wine
1 litre chicken stock
sea salt and freshly ground black pepper
100g unsalted butter, plus 50g extra, at room temperature, for serving
1 red onion, peeled and finely chopped
300g Carnaroli risotto rice
100g Parmesan, grated

Open the wine and put it in a warm place to let it breathe. Bring the stock to the boil, check for seasoning, then turn the heat down to a gentle simmer. Melt the butter in a medium, thick-bottomed, high-sided pan. Add the onion and cook for about 10 minutes over a low heat, until completely soft and lightly golden. Add the rice, turn the heat up slightly, and stir to coat each grain with the buttery mixture until the rice becomes opaque.

Start to add the wine, one ladleful at a time, allowing the first ladleful to go syrupy before adding the next. Add two-thirds of the wine in this way. Stir frequently and do not let the rice stick to the bottom of the pan. Then start to add the stock, again one ladleful at a time, until the rice is al dente, letting each ladleful be absorbed before you add any more. You may not need to use all the stock.

To finish, add the remaining wine and let it be absorbed into the risotto. Take the pan off the heat and add the 50g of softened butter and half the Parmesan. Stir well and serve in warm bowls, with the remaining Parmesan on the side.

Coarse-grained white and yellow polenta

Set polenta

ing polenta

Pour the polenta on to a plate for setting

ed, wet and fried polenta

POLENTA MORBIDA

SOFT POLENTA

For 6–8

350g polenta flour, medium ground
1.75 litres water
sea salt and freshly ground black pepper
extra virgin olive oil
150g butter
200g Parmesan, freshly grated

Put the polenta flour into a jug so that it can be poured in a steady stream.

Pour 1.5 litres of water into a medium, thick-bottomed pan and add 1 teaspoon of salt. Lower the heat to a simmer and slowly add the polenta flour, stirring with a whisk until completely blended. The polenta will thicken quickly and bubble volcanically. Reduce the heat to as low as possible and cook, stirring from time to time with a wooden spoon, for 30–40 minutes, or until the polenta falls away from the sides of the pan and has become very thick.

When ready, transfer the polenta to a large flat baking tray or plate and spread out to form a cake about 2cm thick. Leave until completely cold, then cut into wedges or slices.

POLENTA CON VINO BIANCO

SOFT POLENTA WITH WHITE WINE

For 6–8

350g polenta flour, medium ground
1.5 litres water
sea salt and freshly ground black pepper
150ml white wine
extra virgin olive oil

Make the polenta as described in the polenta morbida recipe, adding the wine to the pan with 3 tablespoons of olive oil. Season to taste.

POLENTA AI FERRI

GRILLED POLENTA

For 6–8

350g polenta flour, medium ground

1.75 litres water

sea salt and freshly ground black pepper

extra virgin olive oil

Make the polenta as described in the polenta morbida recipe, omitting the butter and Parmesan. When ready, transfer the polenta to a large flat baking tray or plate and spread out to form a cake about 2cm thick. Leave until completely cold, then cut into wedges or slices.

Preheat a griddle pan or barbecue until very hot. Season the slices well and grill on each side until crisp and brown. Do this in batches, keeping the polenta hot in a warm tray.

POLENTA FRITTA

FRIED POLENTA

For 6–8

350g polenta flour, medium ground

1.75 litres water

sea salt and freshly ground black pepper

extra virgin olive oil

Make the polenta as described in the polenta morbida recipe above, omitting the butter and Parmesan and not adding the black pepper at this stage.

When ready, transfer the polenta to a large, flat baking tray or plate and spread out to form a cake about 2cm thick. Leave until completely cold, then cut into irregular shapes.

In a generous frying pan, heat 2 tablespoons of olive oil. When the oil is very hot, add the polenta in batches and cook for a few minutes until golden brown. Turn over, season with salt and pepper, and cook for a further few minutes. Drain on kitchen paper and keep warm.

BREADS & PIZZA

BREADS & PIZZA

We can't imagine what Italian food would be like without bread. It is at the heart of Italy's culture, and every region has its own particular types.

At the River Café we use a Pugliese sourdough loaf for making bruschette and soup. This bread contains semolina flour, is a beautiful straw colour and is made in large loaves, often weighing up to two kilos. Traditionally one loaf would last a family a week, its thick, crisp crust surrounding a tough, crumbly but moist interior. Ciabatta is a bread we serve and and cook with. It is a light airy loaf made with yeast and olive oil, excellent for making breadcrumbs and just the correct texture and size to cut into crostini.

In nearly every Tuscan restaurant, crostini are served as soon as you sit down – to be eaten slowly while choosing wine and food, keeping hunger at bay. Included in this chapter is, in our opinion, simply the best chicken liver crostini recipe we know.

Grissini are light crispy breadsticks which originate from Turin and are also served at the start of the meal. Making your own grissini is very satisfying provided you get the very stretchy, oily dough to a loose consistency that you can control when shaping the sticks to give them a rustic character when you drop them on to the baking sheet. We have only just started to make our own grissini, as we have a new wood oven at the River Café. This is the ideal oven to cook them in, as it bakes the grissini unevenly and gives them a delicious woody flavour. In the absence of a wood oven, you can still achieve excellent rustic results by using a baking stone in your domestic oven.

All over Italy you will find focaccia, the yeast-based flat bread which originates from Liguria. Made with a similar dough to pizza, it is baked in a stone oven or hearth. Around Genoa, where it is made to be eaten at the table rather than as a street snack, the focaccia is flattened and shaped by hand, giving it the signature dimples, and baked with a generous amount of olive oil poured over. Focaccia col formaggio, made only in and around the village of Recco, is unusual, as it is made without yeast and is baked like a pie, with Crescenza, a sharp, fresh melting cheese, inside. As Crescenza can be hard to find, we use Stracchino for the recipe. It is similar, with a slightly sweeter taste, and it oozes delightfully as you bite into the warm crust. In the south of Italy where it is a very popular and inexpensive street food, the focaccia is made covered with potatoes, more like a pizza.

In Tuscany and Umbria focaccia may be called schiacciata, and there is a famous sweet version, schiacciata con l'uva, which is the breadmakers' celebration of the wine harvest made only during September and October. In this variation, the grapes are scattered over the dough with fennel seeds and as the schiacciata bakes the grapes burst and the juices become absorbed into the bread, a very special sweet treat (see page 120). In Venice at Easter they make a sweet version of focaccia called fugassa, with a dough that includes eggs and butter.

In this chapter on bread we had to include our version of the famous Harry's Bar croque monsieur, a treat we make a beeline for every time we go to Venice. We sit at the bar, watch the barmen make their Bellinis (see page 347) and eat this divine fried cheese and ham sandwich – a reminder of why Italy inspires us so much.

Pizza is sold as a snack all over Italy. We suggest making it at home when you have time and space, as it is fun as well as a challenge. There is great pleasure in making the dough and feeling it come alive in your hands; kneading and stretching it is the traditional way to keep the dough soft and moist, essential for achieving a light crisp crust. Leaving it to rise even for a few extra hours will both deepen the flavour and increase the elasticity. One of the best ways to bake a pizza is directly on the floor of a wood-fired brick oven. The intense heat, which can go as high as 400°C, bakes the dough instantly, both on the top and the bottom. As with grissini, you can achieve a similar result by placing a ceramic baking stone in your domestic oven.

We discovered chickpea farinata years ago, in the markets along the Ligurian coast. It is more of a thick pancake than a bread, eaten warm, straight from makeshift wood ovens. When making it at home, unless you are tempted to buy a farinata pan, use a thick-bottomed ovenproof frying pan and make the batter well in advance, as the perfect farinata needs time for the flour to expand in the water.

As Michelangelo said, 'I feast on wine and bread, and feasts they are.'

GRISSINI

BREADSTICKS

Grissini are very satisfying to make. Be sure your dough is loose enough to allow you to pull them into long sticks by hand, and not to over-bake them — if the flour browns they will become bitter.

For 10
500g Tipo '00' flour
125g semolina flour
50ml extra virgin olive oil
18g fresh yeast, dissolved in 100ml lukewarm water
fine and coarse sea salt
200ml lukewarm water

Mix the flour and semolina with the oil, the yeast mixture and 1 teaspoon of fine sea salt. Slowly add the remaining water to make a soft dough. Knead for 5–10 minutes, until stretchy and soft. Add more flour if the dough is too sticky.

Shape into 6 oblongs and leave to rise on an oiled tray in a warm place for 1 hour.

Preheat the oven to 180°C. Take one of the dough oblongs and carefully transfer it to a board. Cut off 1.5cm thick pieces of dough and stretch them with your hands to form long breadsticks. Continue until all your dough is used up.

Place the grissini on flat trays lined with baking parchment, sprinkled with a little coarse sea salt, and bake in the oven for about 30–35 minutes, until light brown and completely dry.

Breadsticks and focaccia with salt

CARTA DA MUSICA

SARDINIAN FLATBREAD

Carta da musica, or flatbread, originated in Sardinia and is made throughout the island. It is crispy, as thin as the paper it is named after. It is both enjoyable and easy to make, and lasts for a long time, wrapped in greaseproof paper and kept in an airtight tin.

Makes 8–10

650g fine semolina flour
100g plain flour
18g fresh baker's yeast, dissolved in 100ml lukewarm water
600ml water
1 teaspoon fine sea salt

Mix all the ingredients in a large bowl to form a soft dough. Shape into golfball-sized balls and leave to prove for 1 hour.

Heat your oven to 230°C, with a pizza stone or thick baking tray placed on the bottom shelf. If possible, use the fan-assisted setting where the heat in the oven comes from the top only. Roll out the balls of dough evenly until you have 2mm thick discs. Place one of the discs on the pizza stone or baking sheet. The disc should immediately puff up. Remove it straight away while still soft. Repeat with all the discs.

Working as quickly as you can, while the breads are still warm, and using a small, serrated knife, cut them along the edge, removing top from bottom, like opening a pitta bread. Stack these discs together and press them down to flatten them. Lower the oven temperature to 180°C and bake them again for 4–5 minutes, until crisp and slightly brown.

FOCACCIA AL SALE

FOCACCIA WITH SALT

Though it is now made all over Italy, focaccia comes from Liguria, where every small village sells slices in its bakeries and grocery stores. It is an olive-oil-based salted dough, which may be either plain or topped with rosemary, potatoes and olive oil.

For 10

750g Tipo '00' flour

1 tablespoon finely ground sea salt, plus extra (not ground) for scattering over the top

25g fresh yeast

150ml extra virgin olive oil, plus extra 50ml or so for cooking

Mix the flour and finely ground salt together on a large board and make a well in the centre. Crumble the yeast into a cup of water at room temperature, not too hot, and stir. How much more water you need now will vary depending on the type of flour you use. Pour the yeasty water into the well in the flour, along with the oil, and refill the cup with water.

Begin to mix with one hand, keeping the other clean for the moment. There will not be enough moisture to make a cohesive dough, so, bit by bit, add more water until you can knead it. The object is to have a very soft and pliable dough. Add extra scatterings of flour if it is too sticky, and wet your hands with water if it is too firm. Knead for about 10 minutes.

Leave the dough for about an hour, covered, in a warm place, until doubled in size.

Lightly oil an oven tray, about 25 x 35cm. When the dough has risen, roll it out to fit into this tray and brush it lightly with oil to keep it from drying out during its second proving, which should take about 30 minutes. Then, with the points of your fingers, dimple the sheet of dough, leaving a border of 1cm around the edge, and let it prove again for another 20–30 minutes.

Heat the oven to 200°C. Sprinkle coarse sea salt over the focaccia. Mix another 50ml or so of oil with 50ml water in a jar and pour this over the focaccia before putting in the oven. This seems strange, but the water helps to keep the dough soft and moist in some of the grooves, which is a nice quality. The focaccia is ready after about 25 minutes, when it is a golden colour.

FOCACCIA COL FORMAGGIO

FOCACCIA WITH CHEESE

This recipe originates from the village of Recco in Liguria. Now, you will also find that focaccia col formaggio is made in many of the restaurants and bakeries all along the coast, from Genoa to La Spezia. Served hot, this crispy olive-oil-flavoured focaccia, with the melted, slightly sour cheese, Stracchino, and the flavours of the wood oven, is something not to be missed.

For 12
400g plain strong bread flour
sea salt
extra virgin olive oil (Ligurian is ideal)
500g Stracchino

Place a large mixing bowl in a warm place and sieve the flour into it. Add 1 tablespoon of sea salt and 3 tablespoons of olive oil. Stir in 200ml of warm water with a wooden spoon and mix together until you have a sticky dough, then cover with a cloth and leave in a warm place for 30 minutes.

Tip the dough on to a generously floured work surface. Coat your hands with flour and knead it for several minutes until it becomes smooth and elastic. Divide the dough into two, place in separate bowls, cover both with clingfilm and leave for 15 minutes.

Preheat the oven to 225°C. Flour the surface again and roll out the first ball as thinly as possible into a 40cm diameter disc. Lightly oil a flat baking tray or pizza pan and lay the dough down on it carefully. Grate or thinly slice the Stracchino over so that it covers the surface of the dough to within 1cm of the edge. Scatter with sea salt.

Roll out the second ball of dough to the same size. Place it on top of the first one to cover the cheese, and press it down lightly at the edges. Drizzle the surface with olive oil, scatter with sea salt and place in the oven for 25 minutes, or until the crust is light brown. Cut into wedges while still warm.

SCHIACCIATA

FOCACCIA WITH BLACK GRAPES

In Italy, desserts and cakes are often fruit-based and dry, like this schiacciata, a flat bread traditionally made during the grape harvest with whichever wine grapes are being harvested. In Tuscany this would be the small Sangiovese grapes. A guest arrived at the house we were staying in with a present of a schiacciata made with sweet table grapes, because the wine grapes were not ripe. We couldn't wait to taste it, so we ate it with our coffee for breakfast. Later we had it as a dessert after lunch and, as it sat on the table during the afternoon, everyone who passed by broke off a piece. By evening it was gone.

For 10

extra virgin olive oil

1kg black grapes

4 tablespoons sugar

4 tablespoons fennel seeds

For the dough

25g fresh yeast

200ml water

4 tablespoons sugar

8 tablespoons extra virgin olive oil

sea salt

500g plain flour

Dissolve the yeast in the water and mix in the sugar, the olive oil and a pinch of salt. Place the flour in a heap on a wide work surface and make a well in the middle. Add the yeast mixture, mix well, and knead for at least 15 minutes. Put into a bowl, cover with a cloth, and let it rise for at least 1 hour.

Preheat the oven to 180°C. Knock back the dough and divide into two. Grease a 30 x 40cm baking tray with olive oil and press out half the dough as thin as possible, making sure there are no holes. Spread with about half the grapes, sprinkle with 2 tablespoons of sugar and 2 tablespoons of fennel seeds, and drizzle with olive oil. Cover with the remaining dough, crimp the edges and spread the remaining grapes, sugar, olive oil and fennel seeds on top. Drizzle with olive oil.

Bake in the oven for 45 minutes, or until very brown and crisp. Remove from the oven and allow to cool before cutting into squares to serve.

FARINATA CON ROSMARINO

CHICKPEA FARINATA WITH FRESH ROSEMARY

From the French border to just south of Genoa, many street markets have a small wood-burning oven with a queue of people lining up to buy a piece of farinata. This chickpea flour 'pancake' is delicious on its own, but at the River Café we serve it with prosciutto or other antipasti.

The traditional pan used for farinata is made from copper and lined with tin. The pan is round, between 30 and 50cm in diameter; the base is thick, and the sides are rounded and only about 1cm high. Most traditional farinata pans won't fit into domestic ovens, but a thick-bottomed frying pan with an ovenproof handle will work just as well.

For 6

1 litre warm water
300g chickpea (gram) flour
sea salt and freshly ground black pepper
approx. 200ml extra virgin olive oil
2 tablespoons chopped fresh rosemary leaves

Pour the water into a large bowl. Sieve in the chickpea flour and whisk until the mixture has a smooth consistency. Add 1 tablespoon of salt and 1 teaspoon of black pepper and stir to combine. Cover with a cloth and leave to rest in a warm place for at least 2 hours.

Preheat your oven to 250°C, or as high as it will go. Skim the foam from the surface of the batter and stir in 100ml of olive oil. Pour 1 tablespoon of oil into a farinata pan, or a frying pan with an ovenproof handle, and place in the hot oven for about 5 minutes, until the oil is smoking.

Give the batter a good stir, then pour just enough into the pan to make a layer approximately 1cm thick, tilting the pan to spread it evenly. Sprinkle a little rosemary over the top and return the farinata to the oven to bake for about 10 minutes. The top should be brown and the pancake should have a crisp texture, but be soft in the centre. Slice into wedges and serve immediately as an appetizer, with a glass of prosecco, while you get on with making the rest of the pancakes – this amount should make 3.

CROSTINI DI CICORIA LUNGA

CROSTINI WITH LONG-LEAF CICORIA

The green long-leaf cicoria is a cultivated variety of the dandelion family. It is grown all over Italy, where you will find it cooked in a variety of ways. In the south it is often combined with chickpeas, white beans and dried broad beans. Cicoria cooks like spinach when boiled in salted water, and the taste is deliciously bitter. It is sold in heads, with the base of the root attached, and the leaves are about 25cm long.

Makes 10

500g cicoria lunga or young green dandelion leaves (in Italian they are called tarassaco)

sea salt

extra virgin olive oil

1 ciabatta loaf, cut diagonally into 1cm thick slices

1 garlic clove, peeled and cut in half

Tear the green part of the leaves away from the cicoria stems and discard if they are too yellow or tough. Keep the stems of the small centre leaves. Wash the leaves thoroughly in two changes of cold water.

Bring a large pan of salted water to the boil and blanch the cicoria leaves until tender – they will take about 10–15 minutes. Test for tenderness and drain in a colander, keeping back a cup of the cooking liquid. Roughly chop the leaves, put into a bowl and season with sea salt. Pour in half the retained cooking water and stir in enough extra virgin olive oil to make a loose luscious pulp.

Grill the ciabatta slices on each side. Rub one side only with the garlic, drizzle that side with olive oil, and pile the cicoria on top. Serve with other crostini or sliced prosciutto.

BURRO DEL CHIANTI

LARDO CROSTINI

Lardo di Colonnata is made from pure pork fat cured with selected herbs and sea salt in marble tubs placed in the caves in the Apuan mountains. The lard is aged for a specific period of six to ten months, and during that time its texture becomes dense, almost like cold butter. Lardo di Colonnata is white with a pink streak. Originally lardo was the quarry worker's sandwich filling, along with tomatoes and raw onions. Toasting the bread improves this simple snack, as the lard melts deliciously when warmed by the hot bread. The recipe we have discovered has developed the idea further by mashing up the lard with garlic, rosemary and spices, to make an excellent, rather eccentric, creamy spread for crostini.

Makes 10

2 tablespoons fresh rosemary leaves

½ tablespoon sea salt

2 garlic cloves, peeled

200g lardo di Colonatta, rind removed, cut into small pieces

2 tablespoons red wine vinegar

freshly ground black pepper

1 dried chilli, crumbled

1 ciabatta loaf, cut diagonally into 1cm thick slices

extra virgin olive oil

Put the rosemary, sea salt and 1 garlic clove into a blender and blend to a paste. Add the lardo and pulse-chop until fully combined, then add the vinegar. Season generously with black pepper and the crushed chilli.

Grill the ciabatta slices on both sides, then rub one side sparingly with the second garlic clove, cut in half. Spread the burro del Chianti thickly over each slice, drizzle with olive oil and serve warm.

Crostini with tomatoes, chicken liver crostini, black olive crostini, crostini with long-leaf cicoria, lardo crostini

CROSTINI WITH TOMATOES

In the summer we make large plates of beautiful fresh tomato crostini, a delicious and informal way to start a long lunch or dinner. These crostini keep everyone happy while the pasta is being cooked – something we never do until everyone is seated at the table.

The most important part of this recipe is choosing the tomatoes. Go to the market and don't be afraid to pick them up and smell them. They should have a ripe, pungent tomato smell – that's the best way to judge if they are ripe and full of flavour.

Makes 10

1kg ripe tomatoes

3 garlic cloves, peeled: 2 finely chopped, 1 cut in half

sea salt and freshly ground black pepper

3 tablespoons extra virgin olive oil

1 tablespoon red wine vinegar

1 ciabatta loaf, cut diagonally into 1cm thick slices

24 fresh basil leaves, torn into small pieces

Chop the tomatoes into small pieces, put into a bowl with the chopped garlic and season generously with sea salt and black pepper. Add the olive oil and red wine vinegar. Toss together, cover with clingfilm and marinate for a few hours, stirring occasionally.

Grill the ciabatta slices on each side. Rub one side only with the cut garlic clove and drizzle with olive oil. Add the basil to the tomatoes and toss well. Check the seasoning and spoon some of the tomato mixture on to each crostino.

CROSTINI DI ZUCCHINI

CROSTINI WITH ZUCCHINI

The creaminess of zucchini cooked this way – achieved by adding water to the zucchini when braised in olive oil – makes them an ideal summer crostini.

Makes 10

450g zucchini

3 tablespoons extra virgin olive oil

2 garlic cloves, peeled: 1 thinly sliced, 1 cut in half

sea salt and freshly ground black pepper

2 tablespoons chopped fresh mint or basil

1 ciabatta loaf, cut diagonally into 1cm thick pieces

Cut the zucchini in half lengthways and then into 2cm pieces.

Heat 2 tablespoons of olive oil in a thick-bottomed pan. Add the zucchini and fry, stirring to coat them with the oil. Add the sliced garlic, season and stir. Lower the heat and cook gently for about 10–15 minutes, until the zucchini are slightly browned. Add 3 tablespoons of hot water and carefully stir, scraping the juices into the zucchini as they cook. After about 5 minutes, when the water is absorbed and the zucchini are soft, add the herbs, slightly mashing the mixture with a fork. Check the seasoning. Leave to cool to room temperature, then drizzle with olive oil.

Grill the slices of ciabatta. Rub one side only with the cut garlic clove. Spoon the zucchini mixture over and serve.

FRIED CHEESE SANDWICH HARRY'S BAR

When in Venice we have to visit Harry's Bar to eat this delicious bar snack and to enjoy watching the barmen make their famous Bellinis.

Makes 6

250g Fontina, or Gruyère, or other melting cheese
1 tablespoon Dijon mustard
2 tablespoons Worcestershire sauce
1 dried red chilli or ¼ teaspoon cayenne pepper
1 egg yolk
3 tablespoons double cream
sea salt
12 slices sourdough bread
6 slices prosciutto crudo, or speck di Val d'Aosta
olive oil

Cut the cheese into small dice and put into a bowl in a warm place for 30 minutes. Mix the mustard with the Worcestershire sauce, and add the chilli or cayenne and the egg yolk. Put the cheese into a food processor and add the cream. Pulse-blend for a few seconds, then stir in the mustard mixture. You should have a smooth thick sauce that will spread easily. Season with sea salt.

Trim the crusts off the bread and spread the cheese mixture over one side of each slice. Lay the prosciutto or speck over 6 of the slices and cover with the remaining slices, cheese side down. Press the sandwiches together firmly and cut each one into 3 pieces.

Heat a large frying pan. Pour in enough oil to cover the surface. When the oil is smoking, add as many sandwiches as will fit. Fry for about 3–4 minutes, until light brown and crisp, then turn over and fry the other side. Drain on kitchen paper. Repeat until all the sandwiches are cooked.

Wrap each sandwich in a paper napkin and serve hot, with a glass of very cold Friulano from Specogna, made with the delicious Tocai grape, or with a fresh white peach Bellini in summer (see page 347).

PIZZETTA DI PATATE CON ACCHIUGE, PEPERONCINO E ORIGANO

POTATO, ANCHOVY, CHILLI AND FRESH OREGANO PIZZA

Makes 8

4 large yellow waxy potatoes, peeled

sea salt and freshly ground black pepper

4 tablespoons fresh oregano leaves, roughly chopped

2 small dried red chillies, crumbled

3 tablespoons extra virgin olive oil, plus extra for drizzling

1 batch of Tuscan pizza dough (see page 136)

24 salted anchovy fillets

Slice the potatoes thinly, ideally using a mandolin. Rinse the slices and dry on kitchen paper. Place the slices in a bowl, season generously, and add two-thirds of the oregano, the dried chilli and 3 tablespoons of olive oil. Mix well to make sure the potato slices are coated with oil and the oregano is equally distributed.

Preheat your oven to 230°C, with a pizza stone or thick baking tray placed on the bottom shelf. If possible, use the fan-assisted setting where the heat in the oven comes from the top only. If you have a wood oven, preheat it to very hot.

Divide the dough into 8 balls and roll each one out into a 25cm disc as described on page 137. Cover each pizza base with a single layer of potatoes, slightly overlapping. Place 3 anchovy fillets on top, season only with pepper, and drizzle with olive oil. Finally scatter with the remaining oregano leaves and place in the oven as described on page 137. Bake for 10–12 minutes, or until the base and the potatoes are cooked through and the edges are crisp. Serve hot.

Potato, mozzarella, caper and basil pizza; potato, anchovy, chilli and fresh oregano pizza

PIZZETTA DI PATATE
CON PROSCIUTTO TOSCANO

TUSCAN POTATO AND PROSCIUTTO PIZZA

Makes 8

4 large yellow waxy potatoes, peeled

sea salt and freshly ground black pepper

extra virgin olive oil

1 batch of Tuscan pizza dough (see page 136)

8 slices Tuscan prosciutto (which should be quite fatty), sliced very thinly

Slice the potatoes very thinly, ideally using a mandolin. Rinse the slices and dry on kitchen paper. Place them in a bowl, season and drizzle over 3 tablespoons of olive oil. Stir to make sure all the potatoes are coated with oil and that they are not stuck together.

Preheat your oven to 230°C, with a pizza stone or thick baking tray placed on the bottom shelf. If possible, use the fan-assisted setting where the heat in the oven comes from the top only. If you have a wood oven, preheat it to very hot.

Divide the dough into 8 pieces and roll each one out into a 25cm disc as described on page 137. Cover each pizza base with a single layer of potatoes, overlapping. Season generously and drizzle with olive oil. Place in the oven as described on page 137 and bake for 8–10 minutes, then place a slice of prosciutto, torn in half, on top of each pizza, over the potatoes, and return to the oven for a minute or so to brown the top and wilt the prosciutto. Serve hot.

PIZZETTA DI PATATE CON MOZZARELLA, CAPPERI E BASILICO

POTATO, MOZZARELLA, CAPER AND BASIL PIZZA

Makes 8

1 x 250g ball of fresh buffalo mozzarella

4 large yellow waxy potatoes, peeled

sea salt and freshly ground black pepper

extra virgin olive oil

1 batch of Tuscan pizza dough (see page 136)

3 tablespoons salted capers, rinsed in a sieve under cold water

24 fresh basil leaves

Break the mozzarella into 2–3cm pieces. Slice the potatoes very thinly, ideally using a mandolin. Rinse the slices and dry on kitchen paper. Put the potato slices into a bowl, season generously, and drizzle over 3 tablespoons of olive oil. Stir to make sure each slice is coated with oil and that they are not stuck together.

Preheat your oven to 230°C, with a pizza stone or thick baking tray placed on the bottom shelf. If possible, use the fan-assisted setting where the heat in the oven comes from the top only. If you have a wood oven, preheat it to very hot.

Divide the dough into 8 balls and roll out into 25cm discs as described on page 137. Cover each pizza base with a single layer of potato slices, slightly overlapping. Dot 3 or 4 pieces of mozzarella on top and scatter over a few capers. Season and drizzle with olive oil.

Place in the oven as described on page 137, and bake for 8–10 minutes. The potatoes should be cooked and the mozzarella melted. Dip the basil leaves in olive oil and lay a few on top of each pizza. Bake for just 1 or 2 minutes longer, or until the edges of the pizza are crisp and the basil has wilted. Serve while very hot, otherwise the mozzarella will go hard.

Tuscan potato and prosciutto pizza

Potato, fresh Pecorino and rosemary pizza

FISH

FISH

In Italy little time is lost between the fishermen returning to shore, the catch being sold, and the fish being served up in local restaurants and nearby homes. In the fish market in San Felice Circeo, south of Rome, the fish arrive three times a day and, as the boats come in, there is always a queue of people. All the fish is gone within half an hour of its arrival. To enter a fish market in Italy is to enter a strange world – an amazing assortment of shelled creatures and gleaming whole fish, some of which are huge, like the blue-fin tuna and the spectacular swordfish, as well as many unrecognizable smaller fish packed into boxes, every shade of silver, pale pink, rusty brown, iridescent turquoise and blue black.

Shellfish are displayed alongside each other, as are polpo, polpetti and moscardini. The larger octopi, having already been beaten to tenderize the tentacles, are sold ready to cook.

Steely blue fish include the much-loved anchovies and sardines, fished in the Ligurian Sea and as far down south as the Tyrrhenian Sea. The tradition of preserving these smaller fish in salt or vinegar arose from the fact that they swim in shoals, so that when there was a catch there would be an abundance in the market that day. The cooks would preserve them to be used when the fish were no longer in season.

There is no better way to cook small, whole, fresh fish than dusted in flour, or lightly coated in batter and deep-fried. The fish cook very quickly, remaining deliciously moist, the flavours enhanced by the crisp coating, which needs nothing more than a sprinkle of sea salt and a squeeze of lemon.

Shellfish are loved by Italians, and many varieties of clams and mussels are cooked on every part of Italy's long and varied coastline. In the north, near Viareggio, we collected tiny clams called talline that were found at the edge of the surf and cleaned them by soaking them in a bucket of salt water, changing the water frequently to get rid of the sand. These clams are delicious cooked in Vermentino, a locally produced white wine. In the south, tomatoes are added to give a little acidity to complement the natural sweetness of the local clams.

In the summer months, baby squid, calamaretti, just over 5cm long and pale pink in colour, are ideal for frying whole and are deliciously tender and succulent. Squid this size are perfect for the inzimino recipe on page 170, which is an unusual combination of greens, grapes and squid. Larger squid are usually served grilled, their bodies opened up and scored before being placed on a very hot grill until they curl up, always accompanied with a sauce made from fresh chilli, sea salt and olive oil – a River Café favourite.

The white fish you see most often in the market are orata, dentice, and branzino, called spigola in some parts of Italy. These are the fish Italians will always choose to cook whole, whether large or small, with minimal intervention, either grilled very simply with a little olive oil and a fragrant fresh herb, or baked whole in salt to really bring out the flavour. A piece of lemon is all that is required, for squeezing over. Travelling along the Tuscan coast, we often eat in restaurants where large fish are baked whole over sliced potatoes. In the mushroom season porcini may be sparsely added and, in the winter, sweet fennel. The fish is always brought to the table and filleted with great skill.

When fish is fresh it has virtually no smell except that of the sea. The eyes are bright and clear, the gills crimson and wet, the body stiff. The scales, if there are any, should be shiny, lightly connected to each other and to the body of the fish. To fillet a large white fish such as a sea bass, prepare it by snipping off the side and back fins with a strong pair of scissors. Using a fish scaler, or a large, strong knife, scrape off the scales – this is best done by holding the fish by the tail in a sink and scraping downwards. It is essential to do this thoroughly. Gut the fish by running a sharp knife up from the base of the belly to the head. Remove the guts and wash the fish well. To cut into fillets, lay the fish on its side and, using a sharp filleting knife, carefully slice along the backbone, from tail to head, keeping close to the bones with the blade so as not to waste any of the flesh. Then cut downwards towards the head, which will enable you to remove the fillet. Repeat this with the other side of the fish.

In Italian markets you will also find salted and dried cod, which comes from the cold seas off the coast of Norway. The more common baccalà, which is cod that has been split open and salted, is favoured by most Italian cooks apart from the Venetians, who prefer stoccafisso. Stoccafisso is also cod, preserved not by using salt but by being wind-dried until stiff as a board, a method of curing that is hundreds of years old. Both these products have been part of the Italian larder for centuries, and there are as many recipes as there are regions. Baccalà cooked in olive oil with tomatoes, potatoes and olives is common throughout Italy, but it is around Venice that you will find the confusingly named baccalà mantecato, traditionally made with stoccafisso, a marvellous creamy concoction of pounded fish with olive oil and garlic that is often served on little slices of grilled polenta to accompany a glass of prosecco. We have tried many recipes, and have included one here that transports us, when we eat it, straight into the market at the Rialto bridge in Venice.

White are wild sea bass, large
bream, red mullet and John Dory

PESCE INTERO AL FORNO

PESCE AL SALE

FISH IN SALT

In the restaurant we bake the bigger fish such as turbot, sea bass and salmon in salt, but this is more difficult at home unless you have an oven big enough to take a large, wide baking tray. Wild salmon are rarely small enough to cook whole in this way. A medium-sized salmon will weigh two kilos and feed up to six people. Smaller turbot, John Dory, red mullet and the bream family all bake successfully in salt. The most important factors when choosing a fish are that the gills are red, the eyes are bright, the scales are firm and the head, fins and tail are intact. Make sure you buy enough coarse sea salt – you need at least double the weight of the fish you plan to bake.

For 2

a sprig of fresh thyme, rosemary or myrtle

1 x 500g red mullet, sea bream, sea bass or Dover sole, gutted, head, tail, fins and scales kept on, and gills removed

sea salt and freshly ground black pepper

1.3kg coarse sea salt

180ml water

Preheat your oven to 240°C, or as high as it will go. Put the herb sprig inside the cavity of the fish and season generously with sea salt and black pepper.

Mix the coarse sea salt with the water in a bowl and make a 1cm layer of the mixture in an ovenproof baking tray. Place the fish on top and cover it with more salt, piling it over to coat the fish with a layer 1cm thick. Pat the salt over the fish carefully, following its shape.

Place in the oven and bake for 15 minutes, then take it out and leave it in its salt for about 5 minutes, until cool enough to handle. Break open the salt crust and remove the fish to a warm serving plate.

Serve with salsa verde (see page 394).

PESCE ALL' ACQUA PAZZA

FISH IN CRAZY WATER

At its most basic, this is whole fish cooked in water with salt, garlic, chilli and parsley. The name 'acqua pazza', literally translated as 'crazy water', has always seemed to refer to the chillies making the water 'crazy', but another theory is that the word refers to the fishermen who used seawater to cook it with. Whatever the basis for the name, acqua pazza is a delicious and simple recipe. Do not be tempted to use fish fillets, as a whole fish makes a broth with a stronger flavour, and this is not a fish soup but a whole fish cooked in broth.

Though clams are the most traditional shellfish added to acqua pazza, we also like it with langoustines, scallops or mussels. When in season use fresh tomatoes, but otherwise use a tin of peeled plum tomatoes: drain them, cut them in half lengthways and squeeze out the juice. Though purists will argue that acqua pazza is made only with water, a splash of wine is a delicious addition.

For 2

3 garlic cloves, peeled: 1 thinly sliced, 1 cut in half

4 tablespoons chopped fresh flat-leaf parsley

sea salt and freshly ground black pepper

6 cherry tomatoes, or 2 fresh or tinned plum tomatoes

2 dried red chillies, crushed

2 whole red mullet, 300g each

white wine, optional

4 scallops, langoustines, mussels or clams

extra virgin olive oil

2 slices of ciabatta bread, cut 1cm thick

1 lemon, halved

In a pan large enough to hold the fish in one layer, combine 500ml of water with the sliced garlic, parsley, salt, pepper, tomatoes and chillies. Boil for 5 minutes. Add the mullet and a splash of wine. Cover the pan and cook for about 6 minutes, then carefully turn the fish over, add the shellfish, and cook for a further 6 minutes or until the mullet are just cooked. Season, and drizzle over the olive oil.

Toast the bread, rub gently with the halved garlic on one side, and place on a plate. Add the fish and shellfish, spooning over the tomatoes and broth. Serve with lemon halves.

PESCE MISTO AI FERRI

MIXED GRILLED FISH

Your choice of what fish to grill on the day will come only from a visit to the market. There, you can pick for yourself one larger fish, sea bream or bass, weighing about a kilo, plus a few smaller ones. We try to buy the small mullet, as they have the most delicious flavour, but there are many other fish that are suitable for grilling, and it is up to you to find out from the stallholder which ones are best that day. We like to include some shellfish; in Italy, there are quite a few varieties of fresh prawns, depending on which part of the coast your fish is coming from. Red prawns from the east are always good, as are langoustines; their flesh has a sweet taste and a firm texture. If the baby squid and octopus look fresh, buy those – they benefit from being cooked very quickly on a hot grill and need no more than a squeeze of lemon.

For 8
1 sea bream, weighing 800g–1kg
4 small red mullet, approx. 150g each
sea salt and freshly ground black pepper
5–6 sprigs of fresh rosemary
16 fresh red prawns or small tiger prawns
8 langoustines
juice of 1 lemon
extra virgin olive oil

Preheat a grill until it is very hot, or light a barbecue and let it burn until the coals are glowing and there are no flames. Lightly rub the bars of the grill with oil so that the fish will not stick.

Scale and gut the fish. Season the cavities with sea salt and pepper, and push a sprig of rosemary into each one. Season the outside of the fish and place on the grill. Put the sea bream on first, turning it over after a few minutes when the skin has begun to brown. At this point, put the mullet on the grill and brown on each side; they cook very quickly. Finally put on the prawns and langoustines, grilling just long enough to brown and crisp the skin. Everybody's fish will be different in terms of how long they take to cook, but just keep checking them and remove them from the grill as soon as they are done. As each fish is cooked, remove it to a large, warmed serving plate. Squeeze over a little lemon juice and drizzle with a little olive oil, and keep warm while you finish grilling the rest.

POLPO IN UMIDO

OCTOPUS COOKED IN CHIANTI CLASSICO

Of the many varieties of octopus available in Mediterranean markets, the best and most tender have double rows of suckers on the tentacles. The frozen octopus sold in shops will usually be this kind; it will take up to two hours to defrost, but freezing the octopus seems to tenderize it.

For 4–6

1 x 1–1.5kg octopus, defrosted

1 fennel bulb, cut into quarters

1 small bunch of fennel herb/stalks and leaves

6 bay leaves

2 small bunches of fresh thyme

2 sprigs of fresh sage

1 head of garlic, cloves peeled and each one cut in half

1 bottle of Chianti Classico

5 whole red chillies

5 fresh plum tomatoes, or drained tinned ones

sea salt and whole black peppercorns

1 teaspoon fennel seeds

extra virgin olive oil

½ a sourdough loaf, cut into 1cm thick slices

Place the octopus in a large, wide, thick-bottomed lidded pan. Cover with the wine and top up with a little water to make sure the octopus is completely covered with liquid. Add all but 2 of the garlic cloves, and the chillies, herbs, fennel and tomatoes. Season with a tablespoon of sea salt, a teaspoon of peppercorns and the fennel seeds. Bring slowly to the boil, then turn the heat down, partially cover the pan, and simmer gently for 2–3 hours, during which time some of the liquid will be absorbed. Add a drizzle of olive oil to moisten the octopus as it becomes exposed to the air. Test for tenderness by squeezing one of the tentacles. They should feel soft and giving. Leave the octopus to cool to room temperature in its juices.

When ready to serve, grill the bread on both sides, rub one side with the reserved garlic and drizzle with extra virgin olive oil. Cut the octopus into 3–4cm pieces and spoon them on to the bruschetta. Add a few of the herbs and a piece of chilli from the pan, drizzle with more olive oil. Lovely served with a wedge of lemon.

MAZZANCOLLE CRUDE

LANGOUSTINE CARPACCIO

Sweet Ligurian olive oil is the oil to drizzle over raw fish. It is important to buy live langoustines to make this.

For 4

20 fresh live langoustines
sea salt and freshly ground black pepper
1 dried chilli, crumbled
extra virgin olive oil
2 lemons

Put your serving plates into the fridge 20 minutes before you want to serve the langoustines.

Place the live langoustines on a board so that the belly side is facing you, holding them carefully, with your hand protected by a cloth or glove. Cut down the centre to butterfly them open. Place them side by side on a serving dish sprinkled with salt, pepper and crumbled chilli.

Drizzle generously with olive oil and serve immediately, with wedges of lemon, on your cold plates.

Raw langoustine is a delicacy that is now prepared by Italy's seafood cooks, using the large, fleshy crustaceans that slip down the throat like oysters

Boiled octopus with potatoes

INZIMINO DI CALAMARI

SQUID WITH RED WINE, CHARD AND GRAPES

Inzimino is a Tuscan stew cooked with squid or cuttlefish, chard and sometimes chickpeas. This recipe comes from Bolgheri, on the Tuscan coast, and it was made using the grapes grown on the Ornalia estate.

For 8
500g small squid
extra virgin olive oil
3 garlic cloves, peeled: 2 roughly chopped, 1 left whole
sea salt and freshly ground black pepper
1 dried red chilli, crumbled
150ml Chianti Classico
500g chard leaves, stalks removed
500g red Sangiovese wine grapes, taken from stems
8 slices of sourdough bread

To prepare each squid, hold the body in one hand and, with your other hand, gently pull out the head, tentacles and guts. Try to pull out the flexible, blade-like transparent quill at the same time. Then, with your fingers, extract any remaining pulp. Rinse the body sacs and cut off the side flaps. Cut the hard head off the tentacle section, leaving the tentacles intact, and discard. Wash the tentacles. Cut each body in half at an angle, keeping the tentacles whole.

Slowly heat 3 tablespoons of olive oil in a large flat frying pan. Add the garlic and the squid, season with salt, pepper and chilli, then cover with a tight-fitting lid and cook very gently for 15–20 minutes. Add the wine, lightly cover the pan and leave to cook slowly for an hour, making sure that there is always liquid in the pan and adding a little water or wine if necessary to keep it moist.

Meanwhile roughly chop the chard leaves. When the squid is really soft, cover with the chard and replace the lid. Continue to cook until the chard is tender, about 10 minutes. By this time most of the liquid will have been absorbed. Finally, stir the grapes into the mixture. Keep the pan on the heat briefly, just to warm the grapes through. Test for seasoning and drizzle with extra virgin olive oil.

Grill the bread on both sides and lightly rub one side only with the whole garlic. Spoon the inzimino on to the bruschetta and drizzle over some olive oil.

BACCALÀ MANTECATO

BEATEN DRIED COD

In Venice, away from the crowded areas of San Marco near the Rialto bridge and the wonderful food market, you can discover small bars serving dishes of sardines in salt, marinated aubergines, anchovies, and the most delicious baccalà mantecato on grilled polenta or simple crostini. Traditionally, this was made with stockfish, the dried cod from Norway, and this is still favoured by the Venetians above the baccalà, the salted cod that is more popular with the southern Italians and is possibly easier to source for this recipe.

For 4

500g baccalà or stockfish

1 litre milk

250ml extra virgin olive oil, plus extra for serving

2 garlic cloves, peeled and finely chopped

sea salt and freshly ground black pepper

a pinch of dried chillies

1 tablespoon finely chopped fresh flat-leaf parsley

Soak the baccalà, in one piece, in cold water for a minimum of 48 hours, changing the water a few times. If using stockfish, the Italians say that you should soak it for 4 days.

Take the fish out of the water and remove the skin and bones. Place it on a large board and cover it with clingfilm, then beat it with a mallet until it breaks up into small fibrous pieces.

In a thick-bottomed pan, heat the milk to boiling point. Heat 2 tablespoons of olive oil in a large flat pan, add the garlic and let it colour. Season with salt (if using stockfish), pepper and a pinch of dried chilli.

Add the fish and stir it into the garlic and oil, then add the hot milk. Bring back to the boil, then lower the heat and simmer for 2–3 minutes. Remove from the heat and leave to cool. Drain the fish, keeping the liquid. Place the warm fish in a food processor and pulse-chop briefly to break the fish down into a thick paste. Add 2–3 tablespoons of the reserved milk to loosen the mixture, then start to add the olive oil slowly, pulse-blending until the fish has the texture of creamy mashed potato. Test for seasoning.

Serve warm on slices of grilled polenta or crostini, drizzled with olive oil and sprinkled with parsley.

SEPPIA IN UMIDO

STEWED CUTTLEFISH WITH GRILLED POLENTA

For 2

extra virgin olive oil

1 red onion, peeled and sliced

2 garlic cloves, peeled and sliced

3 salted anchovy fillets, rinsed and roughly chopped

1 dried red chilli, crumbled

sea salt and freshly ground black pepper

250g small cuttlefish or squid, cleaned and each cut into 3 or 4 pieces

1 large ripe plum tomato, peeled and roughly chopped

2 tablespoons chopped green fennel tops

125ml Chianti Classico

2 slices of grilled polenta (see page 109), cut 2cm thick

Heat 2 tablespoons of olive oil in a thick-bottomed pan. Add the onion and garlic and gently soften over a low heat for 5–10 minutes. Add the anchovies, season with the chilli and black pepper, and continue stirring just long enough to melt the anchovies. Add the cuttlefish, tomato, fennel tops and wine. Half cover the pan and cook very gently for 45 minutes, or until the cuttlefish is soft to bite and you still have a little juice left in the pan. Test for seasoning – you may need to add salt.

Heat a griddle pan or barbecue until very hot. Lightly brush the polenta with olive oil and season. Place on the grill and cook for about 3–4 minutes on each side, until crispy and brown. To serve, place a slice or two of polenta on each plate and spoon over the cuttlefish along with the juices from the pan.

This is a perfect recipe to make when
you have a slab of polenta left over
from the day before. The richness of the stew
is a contrast to the crispy polenta crust

FRITTO MISTO DI MARE

DEEP-FRIED SMALL MEDITERRANEAN FISH

The tradition of deep-frying spreads right across Italy. In the coastal areas, where really fresh fish is available, you will find fritto misto di mare on every menu. The choice and variety of fish will be not only seasonal but strictly what is available on that day. In Lazio, we enjoyed moscardini, tiny octopus, lightly dusted with flour and sea salt then fried for a few seconds, and in Venice we tried moleca, small soft-shell crabs, also lightly floured and fried, which are found on the menus of the best restaurants. In Liguria, whole anchovies are deep-fried and served piled high on a plate for enjoying communally before the meal. We do the same in the River Café when we can get hold of fresh Mediterranean anchovies.

Most fish stalls in Mediterranean markets sell their daily choice of small fish that are suitable for this recipe. You have to go early in the morning as they sell out very quickly. The day we went, we were lucky enough to find langoustines, soles, mullets, eels, prawns and moscardini.

For 8
350ml milk
2kg mixed small fish, washed and patted dry
250g plain flour (Tipo '00' is best)
sea salt and freshly ground black pepper
1.5 litres sunflower oil
2 lemons, quartered

Pour the milk into a large bowl. Add the fish and leave to soak for 15 minutes. Mix the flour with salt and pepper.

Heat the oil to 180°C in a deep fryer, or use a high-sided, thick-bottomed pan. Remove the fish from the milk and drain off any excess, then dip into the flour so that each fish is lightly coated. Add the fish to the hot oil in batches and fry for about 2 minutes, until light brown and crisp. Remember to reheat the oil to 180°C before the next batch. Drain on kitchen paper and serve immediately with lemon quarters.

MEAT

MEAT

Most of the familiar Italian regional meat dishes have been handed down from generation to generation. The ones we make over and over again are in this chapter – ossobuco, lo stinco, arista fiorentina, peposo, maiale al latte and bollito misto.

Veal is the most prized meat in Italy, found in the cooking of the northern provinces, from Piedmont, through Emilia Romagna, to the Veneto. On this large plain the cows graze on herbs and grass, and their milk is made into delicious butter and the all-important cheese Parmigiano. To produce milk-fed veal, the calves are nurtured with their mothers for three months. This meat has a pale pink flesh, creamy white fat and a fine tender texture, ideal for the much-loved carne cruda di vitello and vitello tonnato. In the Veneto the farmers feed the milk-fed calves on grass as well and rear them for up to eight months. By then the animals have reached a good size, but they are slaughtered before their hormones have developed, so the meat remains sweet and succulent. This liver is most sought after, particularly by Venetians, the kidneys are a perfect size and texture, and the brains are extremely delicate.

Recipes for oxen are not so well known in Italy, as these are used as working animals and so their meat is old and tough. However, in Tuscany, the very large noble white Chianino cattle have always been bred for their unique flavour and texture. Today these prized cattle are still raised in the traditional way, in pastures away from the roads, among the vines and olives, giving the meat the strong, definite flavour enjoyed by the Tuscans. The most well-known cut is the fiorentina, a T-bone steak that includes the sirloin and the fillet, which is always grilled over wood until black on the outside but rare in the middle.

Many of the beef recipes we love to cook are inspired by Dario Cecchini, the butcher in the village of Panzano in Chianti. We will never forget the morning we ate a dish of his peposo, which he had just taken out of the bread oven where it had been gently cooking all night. He served it in bowls with a thick slice of bread – this was the same nourishing dish that Brunelleschi gave his builders in the fourteenth century when they were creating the Duomo in Florence. This extraordinary recipe of beef shin in Chianti, with fistfuls of black pepper and garlic, turns beef to the texture of butter and is one of the most memorable dishes we have ever eaten, particularly as we had it with a glass of red wine on a cold November morning.

Milk-fed lamb and kid are found on menus in the south of Italy. In Rome, the Easter speciality is abbacchio, prepared with lamb butchered at six to eight weeks and weighing only about six kilos. The meat is very pale and tender, with hardly a trace of fat, and the lamb is cooked whole on a spit; the flavour is delicate and every part of the animal is eaten.

Pork is a common centrepiece for festivals, as pigs are easy to rear, small in size, and can be kept near the house and fed on scraps. A pig matures in one year and breeds prolifically – each female pig can have two litters a year. The excellent-tasting meat is preserved in many ways: hams, sausages and salamis. There are also larger sausages such as cotechino, made from the skin and fat and flavoured with spices, and zampone, a stuffed pig's trotter, that are boiled and form an important part of a traditional bollito misto. In Sardinia, baby pigs are roasted whole for several hours over a wood fire made from branches of the myrtle that grows all over the island. This is porchetto, their national dish – not to be confused with porchetta.

Porchetta, traditionally a product of Lazio, is now sold all over Italy as street food. Prepared using a fully grown pig, the body of which has been completely boned, it is stuffed with its own offal, and with herbs such as garlic, fennel and rosemary. The meat is then tied back into shape and slowly roasted for hours in special ovens. It is always served cold, sold from customized vans by the roadside and at festivals and fairs. The person who carves the meat will ask you if you would like crisp crunchy skin, the soft livery stuffing, or the thick juicy slices from the shoulder or loin to fill your panino, a hollow bread bun designed for the purpose of holding together so many meaty bits. There is a special salt, pepper and fennel seed mixture on the counter which you can help yourself to. We have always had our favourite porchetta places, like the one on the Via Aurelia between Pisa and Viareggio, close to the sea, in the middle of a pine wood, which provided a perfect snack for us after we had been on the road all day.

The technique for cooking meat in Italy varies according to the cut, the age, how the animal has been fed and how it has been butchered. A conversation with the butcher is an integral part of shopping in Italy. The way the piece of meat is prepared is vital to the success of the recipe. It is, as with all Italian cooking, the quality of the ingredient that will make the dish exceptional.

PORCHETTA

ROASTED BONED WHOLE PIGLET

Street markets, fairs and lay-bys are where you will find porchetta vans throughout northern Italy. The open-sided vans display beautifully prepared boned whole pigs that have been stuffed and roasted with the typical herbs for flavouring pork — fennel and rosemary — and garlic. The liver, heart and kidneys are usually included as they influence the flavour.

The porchetta is always cut in thick slices and placed inside a panino. In this sandwich you are usually offered a bit of crackling and some of the stuffing. These panini are almost a meal in themselves and are absolutely delicious.

Choose a time when you are having a party if you want to cook porchetta at home, since to be true to the recipe you need a whole pig. We've used a small suckling pig, which is the only way to make it in a home kitchen as it will fit in a domestic oven.

For 10

1 piglet, weighing 8kg, on the bone, with kidneys, heart and liver intact if possible
(or buy 200g chicken livers and 1 pork kidney)

extra virgin olive oil

10 garlic cloves, peeled and finely chopped

1 bottle of white wine

10 sprigs of fresh rosemary: 5 left whole, leaves of 5 picked and finely chopped

3 tablespoons fennel seeds, ground

2 dried red chillies, crumbled

sea salt and freshly ground black pepper

1 head of celery

3 carrots

1 small red onion

3 stalks of fennel

6 bay leaves

Ask your butcher to bone the piglet, keeping the head and trotters intact, i.e. the shoulder bone, ribs, hip and thigh bones removed. Open it up and flatten it out on a large board, skin side down. Trim off some of the lean parts of the shoulder and legs. Chop this meat finely or use a mincer to mince it. Chop the liver, kidneys and heart to the same texture.

Heat a thick-bottomed frying pan and put in 2 tablespoons of olive oil. Add the garlic and cook until golden, then add the chopped pork, liver, heart and kidneys and stir to lightly brown. Add 1 glass of the wine and cook for about 3 minutes. Take off the heat, add the chopped rosemary leaves, fennel seeds and chilli, and season generously – remember, this is the stuffing and is the seasoning for the whole piglet, so the flavours should be strong. Allow this mixture to cool.

Wipe the inside and outside of the piglet with kitchen paper, then place it skin side down on a board. Scatter with sea salt and spread the liver mixture all over the inside. Roll the piglet up, keeping its basic shape; tuck the front trotters forwards and the back trotters back towards the tail. Use butcher's string to tie the whole carcass together at 5cm intervals, like a huge sausage.

Preheat the oven to 220°C. Choose a large roasting tin into which the whole piglet will fit, and drizzle olive oil over the base. Cut the celery into big pieces, peel and cut the carrots into quarters, and cut the onion into eighths. Scatter the vegetables all over the base of the roasting tin and place the fennel stalks, the whole rosemary sprigs and the bay leaves among them. Carefully place the piglet on top (you may have to bend it a little to fit the tin), then pour in another glass of wine, drizzle a little olive oil over the skin, and scatter sea salt over. Wrap foil around the ears and snout to prevent burning.

Place in the oven and roast for 15 minutes, then turn the temperature down to 160°C and continue roasting, basting the meat from time to time, for at least 2½ hours. Use a skewer to test for doneness, piercing the thickest part of the sausage, which is usually the back end. When cooked the skin should be crisp. If it is still a bit leathery, put it back into the oven for 10 minutes at 210°C to crisp it up.

Remove the cooked piglet to a large carving board. Place the roasting tin back on the heat and add the rest of the wine. Bring to the boil and stir to combine the meat juices and vegetables. Cook briefly and taste the juice for seasoning, then drain into a jug. Skim off the fat and discard the vegetables.

Cut the string from the piglet and carve into thick slices right across the back so that each serving gets some of the skin, the meat and the stuffing. Pour the juices over each slice.

Porchetta with fresh bread

MAIALE AL LATTE

PORK COOKED IN MILK

The curdle that results from the slow cooking together of lemon and milk makes a rich sauce.

For 8
3kg shoulder of pork, boned weight
sea salt and freshly ground black pepper
2 tablespoons extra virgin olive oil
1.5 litres full-fat milk
50g butter
5 garlic cloves, peeled and halved
a small handful of fresh sage leaves
2 lemons, rind pared and pith removed

Remove the rind and most of the fat from the pork and generously season the meat. Heat the olive oil in a thick-bottomed pan just large enough to hold the pork. Brown the meat on all sides, then remove it from the pan, pour away the fat and wipe the pan with kitchen paper.

In a separate pan, heat the milk to just below boiling and set aside.

Melt the butter in the original pan. Add the garlic with the sage leaves and, before the garlic begins to colour, return the pork to the pan. Add enough hot milk to come three-quarters of the way up the pork. Bring to the boil, add the lemon rind and reduce the heat.

Place the lid on the pan, slightly askew, and simmer very slowly on top of the stove for at least 3 hours. Test the meat with a skewer or cooking fork to see if it's ready – it should be very soft.

When the pork is cooked, the milk will have curdled into brown nuggets. Carefully remove the meat to a serving plate, slice quickly, and gently spoon over the sauce.

COSTOLETTA DI MAIALE

DOUBLE PORK LOIN CHOP ROASTED WITH ROSEMARY AND LEMON

We love the traditional arista di Montalcino (see page 198), but if there are only two of you this is a delicious way of cooking thick-cut pork chops and having the juicy quality of a large roast when carved.

For 2

1.5kg pork loin on the bone (ask your butcher to remove the rind, leaving a thick layer of fat)
sea salt and freshly ground black pepper
extra virgin olive oil
200ml dry white wine
2 sprigs of fresh rosemary
1 lemon, cut in half

Preheat the oven to 200°C. Season the meat well with sea salt and black pepper. In a thick-bottomed ovenproof frying pan, heat 2 tablespoons of olive oil until very hot and brown the meat on all sides.

Pour the fat out of the pan and put back the pork. Add the wine and bring to the boil, scraping the bottom of the pan. Add the rosemary and put the pan into the oven.

Cook the meat for 10 minutes then turn over, spooning over the juices from the pan. Squeeze the lemon juice over the meat, leaving the lemon halves in the pan. Return to the oven to cook for a further 10 minutes.

Let the meat rest for at least 5 minutes before serving, then put the chops on a board and cut in two, so that each serving has a bone. Spoon over the juices from the pan and serve with cannellini beans (see page 308).

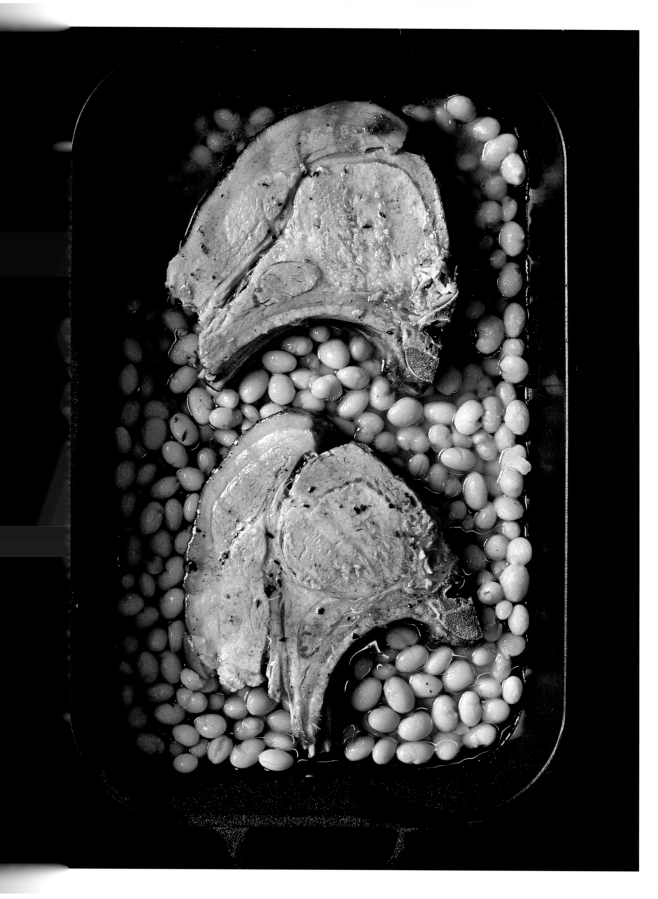

SALSICCE ARROSTO

ROAST ITALIAN SAUSAGES

Italian fresh pure pork sausages are unlike any other sausages. They should contain pure pork meat and coarsely ground fat, mixed with sea salt and sometimes whole black peppercorns. The meat is usually a fatty mixture of cuts from the shins, hocks, neck and belly. These cuts all need slow cooking to get the benefit of the flavour of the pork. In this recipe the fat, which is part of that flavour, is released into the slowly evaporating water in the roasting tin, and then, when all the water has been absorbed, there will be just enough fat left to brown and crisp the skins of the sausages. Try to find Tuscan sausages if you can, or use the more widely available Lucanica sausages.

For 4, or as part of a mixed roast for 8, combined with arista di Montalcino (page 198) and roast pigeon (page 248)

8 Italian fresh pure pork sausages, separated

8 fresh bay leaves

Preheat the oven to 220°C. Place the sausages in one layer in a small roasting tin, one into which they will fit quite snugly. Add the bay leaves and just enough water to cover the sausages, place a piece of foil over the top and put into the oven. Bake for 30 minutes, then remove the foil – at least half the water should have been absorbed by the sausages.

Turn the heat down to 180°C. Continue to roast, uncovered, for up to 30 minutes, until all the liquid has been absorbed and the sausages are colouring in their own fat. This is natural pork fat that is essential in a well-made Italian sausage. During the last 10 minutes of roasting, turn the sausages over to crisp the skin.

Alternatively, you can cook these pure pork sausages on top of the stove. Choose a large deep frying pan, place the sausages in one layer, add the bay leaves and cover with water. Put on a slow heat, partially covered, and simmer until all the water has been absorbed. The final stage is to fry the sausages in the fat that has been released during cooking, to brown and crisp the skin as above.

LO STINCO

ROAST VEAL SHIN

Around the area of Carrara, the mountainous town where the famous Italian marble comes from, there are many simple little countryside trattorias that primarily serve meat dishes. One such restaurant we visited chose a different cut of meat to roast every day of the week, always using cuts that required long slow roasting.

For 4

1 whole veal shin, i.e. the cut used for ossobuco but left in 1 piece (ask your butcher to saw off the knuckle at one end and saw off the end of the bone at the other to expose the bone marrow)

3 tablespoons olive oil

200g unsalted butter

sea salt and freshly ground black pepper

300–400ml Vermentino white wine

6 fresh bay leaves

Preheat the oven to 180°C. If the veal is at all moist, dry it with kitchen paper before cooking. Heat the oil in a thick-bottomed pan that will fit in your oven. Place the veal shin in the pan and brown it on all sides. Remove it from the pan to a bowl to collect any of the moisture that may have started to run. Drain off any remaining oil from the pan.

Add the butter to the pan and return it to the heat. When the butter has melted, add the veal and any juices and season with salt and pepper. When the pan is hot, add 300ml of the wine and the bay leaves. Cover loosely with a piece of buttered parchment and place in the oven.

Slowly roast for 2½ hours, adding more of the wine or some water if the juices dry up. Turn the shin over once or twice during roasting. The meat will become soft and gelatinous and should be served in thick slices, with a little of the bone marrow knocked from the bone on to each serving and a spoonful of juices from the pan.

Veal shin is one of our favourite meats,
roasted whole on the bone,
crisp on the outside, soft like butter
near the bone, carved with a spoon

OSSOBUCO ALLA MILANESE

VEAL SHIN WITH TOMATOES

This dish is served with risotto alla Milanese (see page 96), one of the only times it is acceptable to have risotto accompanying a main course.

For 6

6 pieces of veal shin, 2–3cm thick

sea salt and freshly ground black pepper

50g plain flour, sifted

2 tablespoons olive oil

120g butter

1 small red onion, peeled and finely chopped

2 garlic cloves, peeled and chopped

1 celery heart, finely chopped

½ a bottle of white wine

4 sprigs of fresh thyme

1 x 400g tin of plum tomatoes, drained of juice, coarsely chopped

2 bay leaves

1 x gremolata recipe (see page 204)

Preheat the oven to 150°C. Choose a heavy-bottomed lidded ovenproof pan, large enough to hold the pieces of veal in one layer. Season the veal and dust with the sifted flour, shaking off the excess. Heat the oil in the pan and brown the meat over a moderately high heat, adding more oil as needed. Remove from the pan and set aside. Wipe the pan thoroughly with kitchen paper. Lower the heat, add the butter to the pan and gently fry the onion, garlic and celery for 10–15 minutes, until very soft. Pour in the wine, bring to the boil, and simmer until reduced by half.

Carefully place the ossobuchi back in the pan on top of the vegetables, making sure the bones are placed upright so that the marrow cannot fall out during cooking. Add the thyme, tomatoes and bay leaves. The liquid in the pan should come halfway up the pieces of veal – if it doesn't, add more wine. Bring just to boiling point, then cover with greaseproof paper and the lid, and cook in the lower part of the oven, checking and adjusting the temperature so that the liquid is at a gentle simmer. The total cooking time should be at least 2–2½ hours, after which time the meat should fall from the bone and be tender enough to eat with only a fork. Combine the gremolata ingredients.

Serve the veal with the sauce and vegetables from the pan and sprinkle with the gremolata.

VITELLO TONNATO

COLD VEAL WITH A TUNA AND ANCHOVY MAYONNAISE

Vitello tonnato is common in the cooking of both Piedmont and Lombardy. Poaching the veal is the traditional method, but we often use a piece of leftover roast veal. The sauce can be varied. Some cooks add the meat juices to thin the mayonnaise – we usually toss the slices of veal in their cooking juices and spread the tuna and mayonnaise mixture over the top. The inclusion of smashed anchovies in the mayonnaise, the Piedmontese way, makes this simple dish extremely delicious.

You can make the same dish using cold roast pork instead of veal. It is an excellent summer party dish served as an antipasto or a main course, accompanied by a simple tomato salad.

For a party: 10–15 people

1 x 2.5kg piece of veal rump, with its thin membrane intact

For the poaching liquid

1 head of celery, cut into 5 or 6 pieces

150ml white wine

1 tablespoon black peppercorns

1 red onion, peeled and cut into quarters

3 bay leaves

4 fresh sage leaves

3 sprigs of fresh thyme

2 teaspoons sea salt

For the tuna mayonnaise

12 whole salted anchovies, rinsed and filleted, i.e. 24 fillets

approx. 500ml extra virgin olive oil

2 large free-range organic egg yolks

3 lemons: 2 juiced, 1 sliced

sea salt and freshly ground black pepper

3 tablespoons salted capers, rinsed

2 x 200g tins of tuna, drained of oil

a small bunch of fresh basil, leaves picked

Put all the poaching ingredients into a large pan with 1.5 litres of water and bring to the boil. Add the veal rump, making sure there is enough water to cover it, and bring back to the boil. Skim the surface of any foam, turn the heat to very low, and simmer gently for 1½ hours, or until the rump is cooked through. To test, use a sharp skewer and push it into the middle of the rump, then pull it out and feel the tip of the skewer on your lip; it should be warm. Remove from the heat and allow the veal to cool in the liquid.

Put 12 of the anchovy fillets into a small bowl, drizzle them with a little of the extra virgin olive oil, and set aside. Using a mixer fitted with a balloon whisk, put in the 2 egg yolks and the juice of ½ a lemon, and start to whisk. Start to add the rest of the olive oil in a slow dribble down the side of the bowl, making sure the oil is mixing into the eggs before adding more. Do this until the mixture is very thick. Add the rest of the juice from the first lemon to loosen it up, and carry on adding the oil until you have used most or all of it and you have a full bowl of thick mayonnaise. Season with sea salt.

Chop the rest of the anchovies and put them into another small bowl. Season with black pepper and the juice of the second lemon. Mix well, and stir this mixture into the mayonnaise.

Chop half the capers as finely as possible and add to the mayonnaise. Finally, break the tuna into small pieces and stir these into the mayonnaise as well.

Remove the veal from the broth and finely slice. Lay the slices on large serving plates, covering the plates. Lightly sprinkle with sea salt and black pepper, and drizzle a little of the veal broth over the meat to moisten it. Spread a layer of mayonnaise all over the veal and scatter over the remaining capers. Place the reserved whole anchovy fillets among the capers, sprinkle over the torn basil leaves and serve with slices of lemon.

Cold veal with a tuna and anchovy mayonnaise

BISTECCA ALLA FIORENTINA

BEEF STEAK IN THE STYLE OF FLORENCE

The T-bone, which includes the fillet and sirloin, is a thick-cut steak which when butchered from the Chianino, the largest breed of cattle in the world, will be at least 4cm thick and will feed at least three or four people. These wonderful huge white cattle are farmed in Tuscany.

At the restaurant we are lucky enough to have the choice of Aberdeen Angus or Longhorn beef as an alternative to Chianino. Both of these breeds are much smaller animals, hence the T-bones are smaller, so we get them butchered thicker, maybe 5cm. A steak this size is sufficient for two people.

In Florence and Siena, where these steaks appear on many menus, this highly prized beef with its unique flavour is expensive and is often enjoyed as a family treat on Sundays.

For 6–8

2 T-bone steaks, cut 5–7cm thick

sea salt and freshly ground black pepper

extra virgin olive oil

Take the T-bones out of the fridge and bring them up to room temperature. Trim, leaving a little of the back fat.

There is a debate about seasoning the meat before or after grilling, but all you really need is a well-hung T-bone steak that weighs 2.5–3kg and, ideally, a wood-fired grill. Alternatively, you can use a barbecue or large preheated griddle pan. We season the meat liberally on both sides and grill, turning the meat quite frequently, until it is rare in some parts and better done in others. This will take up to 15 minutes. Leave the meat to rest for 8–10 minutes before carving.

Give each person slices from both the fillet and the sirloin, drizzled with extra virgin olive oil, and serve the bone separately to be enjoyed by enthusiasts.

FILETTO DI MANZO

ROAST BEEF WITH ROSEMARY

We ate roast beef cooked this way, flavoured strongly with fresh rosemary, at a dinner at the Fontodi wine estate in the village of Panzano, in the Chianti Classico region. The Chianino beef was bred by Giovanni Manetti, the owner of Fontodi. His animals, prized for their marbled meat, graze on his land beside the vineyards and olive trees, with rosemary bushes growing all around. This is truly a recipe that brings the best of all these flavours together in the simplest and most exquisite way.

For 6

1kg piece of beef, cut from the thick end of the fillet

sea salt and freshly ground black pepper

10 sprigs of fresh rosemary, each the length of the meat

new season's extra virgin olive oil

1 glass of Chianti

Preheat the oven to 225°C. Trim the fillet, keeping it in one piece, and season it generously all over with sea salt and black pepper.

Make a layer of rosemary on a board, using half the sprigs. Place the fillet on top and cover with the remaining sprigs. Tie with butcher's string to hold the rosemary in place. It should completely cover the fillet.

Choose a small roasting tray that the fillet will fit into quite snugly. Drizzle the tray with olive oil, add the fillet and drizzle more oil over. Place a piece of foil loosely over the top and put into the oven. Roast for 10 minutes, then turn the meat over, add the wine, replace the foil, and return it to the oven. Roast for a further 15 minutes. If the fillet is quite thick, this timing means your meat will be medium rare.

Remove from the oven and let the beef sit in the roasting pan for 5 minutes. Now remove the rosemary and place the meat on a warm serving dish. Strain the juices into a jug and serve the beef cut into slices about 1cm thick, with a little of the wine juices and plenty of the peppery olive oil poured over each.

CARPACCIO DI MANZO

BEEF CARPACCIO

Beef carpaccio was created by Arrigo Cipriani, of Harry's Bar in Venice. The original version, still served there today, has a sauce made with mayonnaise, Worcestershire sauce and lemon juice.

We have adapted the recipe by coating the beef with a crust of black pepper and thyme, then searing it on all sides. Rather than the mayonnaise, we drizzle the beef with extra virgin olive oil, lemon juice and black pepper, then add a few leaves of rocket, which grows in our garden.

We also serve carpaccio with fresh horseradish grated over.

For 6

500g fillet of beef

extra virgin olive oil

sea salt and freshly ground black pepper

1 tablespoon fresh thyme leaves

100g peppery rocket leaves

juice of 1 lemon

Preheat a large griddle pan or chargrill until it is very hot.

Trim the fillet of all fat and sinew and rub it lightly with olive oil. Sprinkle a wooden board with sea salt, black pepper and the thyme leaves, and roll the fillet in these seasonings so that it is coated all over.

Brown the beef on all sides on the griddle pan or chargrill. Do this quickly – you do not want to cook the beef, only to make a crust on the outside. Remove from the heat and leave to cool.

Place the beef on a board and slice it finely, using a very long, sharp knife. Press down on the slices with the flat side of the knife to stretch them.

Put the beef on to 6 plates, still pressing the slices out. Season and drizzle with olive oil. Toss the rocket leaves lightly with oil and lemon juice and lay them over the beef.

BOLLITO MISTO

MIXED BOILED MEATS

Bollito misto is one of the most delicious, complex and sophisticated recipes of traditional northern Italian cooking, and one we cook for a dinner for friends and family, a special occasion or holiday celebration. The excitement of bollito misto is also to do with the sauces you serve with it, which include salsa verde, fresh horseradish and tarragon sauce. Mustard-flavoured preserved fruits, mostarda di Cremona, are always offered too.

The type of meats in bollito misto may vary, but you should always include cotechino sausage and ox tongue. The cotechino, a gelatinous spiced pork sausage, is delicious with the lentils, and the texture of the salt tongue is perfect with the traditional sauces.

The capon is another crucial part of the bollito; it contrasts with the darker, more intense meats, and provides the broth. These free-range chickens are still sold in Italy and can be obtained in some areas of the UK. They are lovely big birds that have an interesting flavour but need a very long slow simmer. It is traditional to serve carrots and celery with bollito, boiled in the broth separately from the meats.

For 12–14

For the meats

2kg beef brisket

2 small veal shins, knuckle bones removed

6 carrots, peeled

3 whole onions: 2 peeled, 1 left unpeeled

1 tablespoon black peppercorns

1 ox tongue, soaked in cold water for 12 hours

4 celery hearts

1 small free-range organic capon, weighing about 4–5kg

1 bay leaf

2 cotechino sausages

For the vegetables

12 carrots, peeled

3 celery hearts, quartered

To serve

1 x lentil recipe (see page 312)

horseradish sauce (see page 397)

tarragon sauce (see page 394)

salsa verde (see page 394)

mostarda di Cremona (available to buy online or in good Italian delicatessens)

Put the beef and the veal shins into a pan with 2 of the carrots, the unpeeled onion and the peppercorns. Cover with cold water, bring to the boil, lower the heat to simmer, and cook for at least 3 hours, skimming the scum from the surface from time to time. At the same time, put the tongue into another pan with a peeled onion, half the celery and 2 more carrots. Cover with cold water and cook until tender, which will also take about 3 hours, skimming the surface from time to time. Before serving you need to remove the skin.

After the tongue and beef have been cooking for 2 hours, put the capon into another pan with 2 more carrots, the remaining celery and onion and the bay leaf. Cover with cold water, bring to the boil and cook very slowly for 1–2 hours, depending on the size of the bird.

Check the cooking time given on the cotechino packaging, then put it, still wrapped, into a pan and cover with water. Bring to the boil, then turn down the heat and simmer for the length of time suggested (the time given will vary according to the manufacturer but should be 30–35 minutes or so).

Clean and peel the 12 carrots. Cut the 3 celery hearts into quarters lengthways. Put some of the capon's poaching broth into a medium pan and bring to the boil. Add the carrots and celery and cook until very tender, about 20 minutes. Set aside.

Carving and serving a bollito for this many people can be an arduous task and is best done by two people. Serve the meats on a large platter with the vegetables and pass round bowls of lentils and the hot stock, as well as the sauces. Alternatively, place portions of each meat on individual plates, ladling the chicken stock over, and add the lentils and vegetables to each plate.

Grilled calves' liver with polenta

POULTRY & GAME

POULTRY & GAME

Italian cooking abounds with classic poultry and game dishes, each region contributing its own traditional touches. It was in the Sant' Ambrogio market in Florence that we were first drawn to the 'polleria', the stall specializing in 'pollame e cacciagione' – chicken and game. There you can find incredible quality, and a vast variety of chicken, ducks, rabbits and guinea fowl, all of which are classified as 'animale da contile', meaning traditional farmyard animals that are fed on a rich diet of kitchen scraps to which corn and oats are added.

The birds and rabbits are usually displayed whole with their heads and feet still attached. The stallholder will hold up the bird for you to inspect and compare, then he will discuss the recipe you have chosen to cook, and only after that will he prepare the bird for you. Shopping this way is such a pleasurable experience: to be able to see clearly how fresh the bird is, the bloom of its skin, and the good colour of the fat, all reflects the pride the Italians have in their produce.

 Rabbits are kept in cages, but are fed on grasses, leaves and wild herbs gathered from the roadsides and vineyards. Animals reared this way have a wonderful flavour, so it is no surprise they are such a popular choice. They are delicious, with juicy, tender white flesh, very different from wild rabbits, which are tough and difficult to cook. In Italy, a plate of jointed rabbit pieces dusted with flour and deep-fried to a crispy brown is often enjoyed as a family treat on special days (see page 253).

The Italians are passionate about hunting. Where we stayed near Lucca, 'cacciatori' (hunters) were always out with their guns at the crack of dawn looking for 'cacciagione' (game birds) found around there – pigeon, pheasant, quail and wild duck from the lakes. It is said that in the old days grouse and partridge were shot as well, but now in most regions these precious birds have now all but disappeared. Italians also love to grill little birds, often with their guts still in, over wood fires: even thrushes have found their way on to the spits.

In Piedmont, the hills and valleys are home to wild game, outstanding wines, wild mushrooms and truffles. The cooking there is rich and inventive and in October and November, when game is in season, you will find dishes with all these ingredients. Our recipe for roast pheasant wrapped in prosciutto, cooked in white wine, with cream and brandy (see page 236), finished with shaved white truffle, was first eaten years ago on a wine trip with our chefs in the Belvedere restaurant, in the hilltop town of La Morra. This is a complex and delicious dish that reflects the time of the year and the history and geography of this area.

Many of the recipes we have included here are for birds roasted in an oven. Traditionally, cooks used to pot-roast the birds over a fire, as many households did not have ovens as we do today. Roasting a bird this way, you can see it browning, smell the delicious aromas, hear the sizzling, and can turn it, test it and be attentive to the progress of the cooking. Italians prefer to cook the meat until it falls off the bone and melts in the mouth, and we recommend you try cooking this way too.

FAGIANO CON TARTUFO

PHEASANT WITH PROSCIUTTO, WINE AND WHITE TRUFFLES

In Piedmont, the white truffle season starts in October and you will discover them in nearly every dish offered on a menu. Polenta also comes from this region and is often served with a combination of game birds and local wines. Going there at that time of the year to discover this very seasonal cooking is a pleasure.

For 2
1 hen pheasant
6 sprigs of fresh thyme
2 garlic cloves, peeled
25g unsalted butter
sea salt and freshly ground black pepper
100g slices of prosciutto, with plenty of fat
100ml white wine
50ml brandy
3 tablespoons double cream
40g white truffles

Preheat the oven to 220°C. Wipe the cavity of the pheasant and pull away any excess fat. Push in the thyme, garlic and butter, and season generously.

Lay the prosciutto slices over the breast of the bird, overlapping them to make a thick coat. Choose a casserole dish or ovenproof pan with a tight-fitting lid. Put in the pheasant, breast side up, and add the wine. Half cover with the lid and place in the oven.

Roast for 30 minutes, then remove from the oven and turn the bird over on to its breast. Return it to the oven and roast for a further 20 minutes, or until the legs pull away from the body and the juices run clear. Remove from the oven again, add the brandy, and leave for 5 minutes for the flavours to combine.

To serve, stir the cream into the juices in the pan and grate in the truffles. Carve the bird, place some of the crispy prosciutto over each serving, and pour over the truffle sauce. This dish is traditionally served with soft polenta (see page 108).

Mixed roast game birds

FARAONA CON GRAPPA

GUINEA FOWL ROASTED IN A POT WITH JUNIPER AND GRAPPA

In Tuscany in August there is not much game about and local butchers offer only guinea fowl and pigeon. Luckily there were fresh branches of juniper berries for us to cook with.

For 2–3

1 large free-range guinea fowl

sea salt and freshly ground black pepper

6 thin slices of pancetta

a bunch of fresh sage, leaves picked, plus 2 whole sprigs

2 tablespoons juniper berries

100ml grappa

1 lemon, halved

extra virgin olive oil

200ml white wine

Preheat the oven to 200°C. Wipe the inside of the guinea fowl and pull away any fat inside the cavity. Season the inside of the cavity well with salt and pepper. Cut 4 of the pancetta slices into matchsticks and put into a bowl. Roughly chop the sage leaves and add to the bowl. Squash two-thirds of the juniper berries in a pestle and mortar and add to the bowl. Push this mixture into the cavity of the guinea fowl and spoon in 2 tablespoons of grappa. Rub the lemon over the skin of the bird, squeeze over the juice, and sprinkle with sea salt. Place the remaining pancetta slices over the breast of the bird and tie in place with string.

Choose a casserole dish or thick-bottomed ovenproof pan with handles and a well-fitting lid. Place the guinea fowl in the dish, breast side down, and add 2 tablespoons of olive oil, half the white wine, and the rest of the grappa. Scatter with the remaining whole juniper berries and place the sage sprigs on either side of the bird.

Take a square of baking parchment at least 5cm wider than the casserole dish and scrunch it up. Open it out and cover the guinea fowl, tucking the edge of the paper down around the bird. Put the lid on and roast in the oven for around 30 minutes, then remove the dish and turn the bird so that it is breast side up. Add the remaining wine. Replace the paper but not the lid, reduce the oven heat to 180°C, and put back into the oven for a further 30–40 minutes, or until the leg juices run clear. Take the guinea fowl out of the oven and let it rest for 10 minutes, and serve with the juices from the casserole and a few of the juniper berries.

PICCIONI

ROAST PIGEON STUFFED WITH THYME AND GARLIC

The meat of young reared pigeons, known as piccioni, is both tender and full of flavour, unlike the wild wood pigeons, now almost disappeared, whose flesh is dark in colour with a flavour both gamey and like liver. Piccioni are usually sold alongside guinea fowl and rabbit. If you do come across wild pigeon, choose only young birds if you wish to make them part of an arrosto misto. In Italian palomba is the name for wild pigeon.

For 4, or as part of a mixed roast for 8, combined with arista di Montalcino (page 198) and salsicce arrosto (page 201)

4 pigeons

4 garlic cloves, peeled, plus one whole bulb, cut across in half

5 bunches of fresh thyme

200g butter

extra virgin olive oil

200ml Chianti Classico

sea salt and freshly ground black pepper

Preheat the oven to 220°C. Season the cavity of each pigeon and push a garlic clove, a sprig of thyme and a knob of butter inside each one.

Place the pigeons close together, breast side up, in a roasting pan with high sides. Dot the remaining butter over and scatter with the rest of the thyme. Drizzle with olive oil and pour in 100ml of Chianti. Cover loosely with foil and roast for 10 minutes, then turn the oven down to 180°C. Remove the roasting pan from the oven and discard the foil. Turn the birds over and add the rest of the Chianti, then roast for a further 30 minutes, uncovered. The birds will be cooked through, which is the Tuscan way, and should rest in their juices in the pan for 10 minutes before serving.

POLLO CON OLIVE NERE

CHICKEN STUFFED WITH OLIVES AND TOMATOES

For 4

1 free-range organic chicken, weighing 2kg

2 lemons, halved

120g black Taggiasca or Niçoise olives, sold in brine

250g large beef tomatoes, cored and cut into 3cm pieces

freshly ground black pepper

extra virgin olive oil

10 sprigs of fresh flat-leaf parsley, leaves picked and roughly chopped (keep some of the stalks)

8 garlic cloves, peeled and halved if large

sea salt

Remove the chicken from the fridge and bring it to room temperature. Pull out any excess fat from the inside and remove the giblets, if there are any. Wipe the inside of the bird and season the cavity generously. Squeeze in the juice from one of the lemon halves.

Wash the brine from the olives and stone them. Put most of the olives and half the tomato pieces into a bowl, season with pepper only, and add 2 tablespoons of olive oil and the juice from 1 lemon, keeping back 1 tablespoonful. Add the parsley leaves and half the garlic. Mix well. Preheat the oven to 210°C.

Spoon most of the mixture into the cavity of the chicken. Push in the remaining lemon half and a few of the parsley stalks. Pour over the reserved tablespoon of lemon juice and rub it into the skin of the chicken. Sprinkle with a little sea salt.

Choose a medium roasting tin into which the chicken will fit quite snugly, and place the bird in the tin breast-side down. Scatter the remaining mixture, along with the rest of the olives, garlic, tomatoes and parsley stalks, around the chicken, and drizzle again with olive oil. Place in the oven to roast for 25 minutes, then reduce the oven temperature to 180°C. Turn the chicken over, baste the breast and stir the tomatoes and olives. Continue to roast for a further 40–60 minutes, until the chicken is cooked through. The best way of testing is to pull the leg gently away from the body – the leg joint should come away easily and you can see if the juices are clear, not bloody.

Rest the chicken for 10 minutes in the roasting tin; this allows the meat to relax before you start carving. Remove the chicken from the pan to a warm serving plate and spoon over the olives, tomatoes and juices from the pan.

In Tuscany, olives, garlic and tomatoes
are often used when cooking rabbit
and chicken. This is a summer recipe,
using the delicious beef tomatoes that
are ready towards the end of the season

POLLO DISOSSATO

SPATCHCOCKED CHICKEN MARINATED IN BLACK PEPPER

If you are asking your butcher to spatchcock your chicken, explain that you want all the bones removed – often butchers will take out only the back and breastbones and leave the bones in the legs and wings. The grilling time in this recipe is so brief because of the way the marinade changes the texture of the chicken. It is vital to cook it quite quickly, otherwise it will be dry.

For 4

1 free-range organic chicken, weighing 2kg

3 tablespoons black peppercorns

2 lemons: 1 zested and juiced, 1 to squeeze over at the end

3 teaspoons sea salt

4 tablespoons extra virgin olive oil, plus extra for drizzling

To spatchcock a chicken you need a small sharp boning knife and a large chopping board. Run the knife down the centre of the breastbone. Ease away the breast up to the wishbone. Cut through the joint where the thigh bone joins the body carcass and pull the leg away, making sure the skin is still intact. Do the same with the wing joint. Repeat, then carefully release the carcass from the skin on the back of the bird so that you are left with a flattened chicken with leg and wing bones still in. Make a slit up the drumstick and thigh on the inside and cut out the bone, keeping the skin intact and connected to the boned outer body. Cut the tips off the wings. Remove only the bone from the wing piece nearest the breast, leaving the bone in the other piece. Trim off any extra fat and skin.

Lay the chicken out flat, skin side down, on an oven tray and scatter over half the peppercorns, half the lemon zest and half the sea salt. Turn the chicken over and scatter over the remaining peppercorns, lemon zest and sea salt. Pour over the lemon juice and 4 tablespoons of olive oil. Cover with clingfilm and put into the fridge overnight.

Preheat the barbecue or griddle. Remove the chicken from the fridge and bring to room temperature. Remove from the tray and drain, keeping the marinade. Carefully place the chicken on the grill skin side up and cook over a moderate heat for 5 minutes. Turn the whole bird over so that the skin side is next to the coals. Brush it with the marinade. As it is boned with the fat removed it will cook very quickly, in about 15 minutes. Test by pressing the thickest part or using a skewer – the juices should be clear. Remove to a warm plate and drizzle with a little olive oil and lemon juice. Leave to rest for 5 minutes, then serve cut into thick slices. It will be just as delicious eaten cold.

CONIGLIO FRITTO

FRIED RABBIT MARINATED IN SAGE

As the flavour of rabbit is somewhat bland, we like to marinate the pieces overnight before cooking them. Children love this dish, and they can eat it with their fingers.

For 4
1 farmed rabbit weighing about 1–1.5kg
3 garlic cloves, peeled
sea salt
2 teaspoons fennel seeds
8 fresh sage leaves, washed
1 tablespoon extra virgin olive oil
200ml full-fat milk
250g plain flour
freshly ground black pepper
4 tablespoons sunflower oil
1 lemon, quartered

Cut the rabbit into small pieces on the bone or ask your butcher to do this for you: the hind leg into two, the shoulder and front leg into two, the saddle into three. Put the garlic, 1 teaspoon of sea salt and the fennel seeds into a pestle and mortar and pound them to a rough paste. Tear up the sage leaves and add them, pounding them into the mixture. Stir in the olive oil.

Put the rabbit into a bowl. Add the garlic mixture and rub it into each piece. Pour in the milk, cover, and leave overnight in the fridge to marinate.

When you are ready to cook the rabbit, scatter the flour over a board, season generously with salt and pepper, then take the pieces of rabbit out of the marinade and coat them lightly in the flour.

Heat 4 tablespoons of sunflower oil in a large thick-bottomed frying pan. When hot, add the pieces of rabbit and shallow-fry for about 12–15 minutes, turning them over, until golden brown and crispy. Drain on kitchen paper and serve with wedges of lemon.

A large platter of fried rabbit pieces is something you often see on the table at a festive lunch in Tuscany

VEGETABLES & SALADS

VEGETABLES & SALADS

One of our earliest memories of travelling together in Italy is walking into a restaurant in Rome and being almost overwhelmed by the vision of countless plates of vegetables. There were discs of deep-fried zucchini tossed with dried chilli and vinegar; grilled marinated red and yellow peppers with basil, garlic slivers and salted anchovies; thick slices of aubergine roasted with oregano; and mounds of boiled spinach, cicoria and chard to be dressed at the table with just extra virgin olive oil and fresh lemon. Another vegetable memory is an expedition to Puglia, where our exploring was limited for fear of missing the delicious bowls of chickpeas, roasted tomatoes, wild greens and roasted olives that were served every day for lunch.

In Italy vegetables are considered central to the meal, not just an accompaniment to a main dish. They have their own place on the menu, and might be eaten as an antipasto rather than prosciutto or salami, a primo instead of pasta, risotto or soup, or a secondo as an alternative to meat or fish. Often at home we have a pasta or risotto, followed only by plates of seasonal vegetables cooked in various ways: grilled, braised, boiled or roasted.

Deep-fried vegetables are found in most regions and are especially particular to Rome, where there is still a strong Jewish tradition for cooking artichokes this way. The famous dish carciofi alla Giudea, found in many restaurants in the capital, uses Romanesco artichokes which are the size of cricket balls, recognized by their thick edible stalks, loosely packed leaves and rounded shape. In villages in Tuscany, simple trattorias will serve porcini fritti in the late summer/autumn, and carciofi fritti in the winter and spring. All cooks have their own batter recipes. When we started making deep-fried vegetables we liked Elizabeth David's crisp, light batter the most, which we have adapted over the years (see page 274).

Italy is a vegetable paradise – there are acres of cultivated fields, small family gardens, and wild greens and herbs growing everywhere. Drive around the countryside and you will see cars parked on the road while their owners forage for dandelion greens, wild fennel, asparagus, nettles, hop vines and borage. We once went for a walk in the countryside with a woman who, all her life, had sold her greens in the Florence market and who was unable to walk more than five steps without picking a herb or salad green from the ground.

The vegetable markets in Italy are startling – teeming in the southern cities of Palermo and Naples, hidden under umbrellas in small quiet streets in Rome. The market is a meeting place for people, and it is where the Italian cook starts planning the meal. Going to the vegetable market in Italy may have more of an influence on the menu than a visit to the butcher or the fishmonger, for this is where good cooking begins. Cooking with seasonal vegetables is one of life's great pleasures.

Always choose fresh, firm zucchini, otherwise they may be soft in the centre and full of seeds, which means they will have no taste

Deep-fried zucchini flowers

PORCINI FRITTI

DEEP-FRIED PORCINI MUSHROOMS

For 4

8–10 firm porcini mushrooms

2 tablespoons plain flour – Tipo '00' is best

sea salt and freshly ground black pepper

150ml sunflower oil

1 lemon, quartered

Wipe the porcini clean with a damp cloth and trim off any earthy bits from the stems. Cut each in half through the cap and stem, then cut into quarters through the stem again.

In a bowl, mix the flour with 1 teaspoon of sea salt and 1 teaspoon of black pepper. Add the porcini pieces and toss to make sure they are generously coated.

Heat the sunflower oil in a wide, thick-bottomed pan. Shake the porcini in a sieve to get rid of any excess flour, then add to the hot oil. Fry for about 3–4 minutes, turning the pieces over until they are brown and crisp. Drain on kitchen paper, scatter with sea salt and serve with a wedge of lemon.

POMODORO FIORENTINO AL FORNO

ROAST BEEF TOMATOES

This is a summer recipe that relies on the quality of the tomatoes. Choose only a true beef tomato, such as the Tuscan variety Costoluto Fiorentino. This variety has few seeds, thin skin, lots of flesh and little juice. It is ideal for roasting, as the tomatoes hold together and have a wonderful, concentrated flavour.

For 4

500g large Costoluto Fiorentino tomatoes or other heirloom beef tomatoes, stalks removed

2 garlic cloves, peeled and finely sliced

1 tablespoon thyme leaves

sea salt and freshly ground black pepper

extra virgin olive oil

Preheat the oven to 180°C.

Wash the tomatoes and cut each one in half across the widest part. Place the tomato halves side by side, cut side up, in an ovenproof dish. Push the garlic slices into the flesh of each tomato, then push some thyme leaves into the flesh and scatter the remainder over the top. Season the cut side of each tomato generously with salt and pepper, and drizzle over a little olive oil.

Place in the oven to roast for 20–30 minutes, or until the tomatoes are soft and lightly browned on top. Serve warm with grilled fish, or as part of a summer antipasti.

OLIVE PER CUCINA

ROAST FRESH OLIVES

Years ago, on a wine trip to Puglia with our friend and wine importer David Gleave of Liberty Wines, we were welcomed by the winemaker Francesco Candido, who involved his whole family in cooking a feast. It was October and they had killed one of their own pigs. As we watched them butcher the pig and prepare the various cuts in different ways, we were served fresh olives, which were roasting over the fire in a large black pan. It was the first time we had ever encountered Pasola olives, which are used only for cooking this way. They were large, like quails' eggs, purplish black and incredibly sweet; they burst in your mouth like hot butter and were quite addictive.

Later, a friend who imports vegetables from the Italian market in Milan rang us at the restaurant and said she had seen them and did we want a box? They are available in November and December, and we get them for that short period every year and serve them as in this recipe.

For 6

500g fresh Pugliese olives and uncured olives, washed

120g cherry tomatoes, washed

6 garlic cloves, peeled and kept whole

150ml extra virgin olive oil

sea salt and freshly ground black pepper

Preheat the oven to 220°C. Place the olives, tomatoes and garlic in an ovenproof earthenware dish, pour over the olive oil and season quite generously with salt and pepper. Place in the oven and roast for 20 minutes. The olives will become soft and sweet, and the tomatoes will burst and combine with the oil and the garlic.

Serve these fresh olives warm, with bruschetta or slices of fresh mozzarella, and with the juices from the dish poured over.

ZUCCHINI SCAPECE

MARINATED FRIED ZUCCHINI

This technique of frying an ingredient then marinating it in vinegar has southern Spanish origins. In Italy this method is used mostly for zucchini, though we have eaten aubergines prepared the same way. It is a wonderfully refreshing way to serve zucchini and there are many recipes, varying from cook to cook. We have noticed that in the south of Italy the zucchini are sliced quite thickly and left to dry out in the sun before being fried and added to the marinade, which can also be cooked or fresh. Mint is nearly always the herb used, and garlic – either raw or lightly fried – is essential for bringing out the flavour of the zucchini.

For 4

2 garlic cloves, peeled
500g medium dark-skinned zucchini
extra virgin olive oil
1 dried red chilli, crumbled
sea salt and freshly ground black pepper
2 tablespoons finely sliced fresh mint leaves
2 tablespoons red wine vinegar

Finely chop one of the garlic cloves, and cut the other into 4 pieces. Slice the zucchini diagonally, about 25mm thick, discarding the end. Lay the slices on a tray lined with paper towel and leave for at least 30 minutes for the moisture to come to the surface. Pat dry. The longer you leave the slices, the more effective this process will be. The drier the zucchini, the browner and more beautifully glistening they become when fried.

Pour enough olive oil into a large flat frying pan to easily cover the bottom, and add the 4 pieces of garlic. Gently fry until golden brown, then discard the garlic but keep the oil hot. Add the zucchini to the pan in one layer (you will need to do this in batches) and fry briefly, turning them over to brown on both sides. Remove to drain on kitchen paper, then place on a serving plate and scatter over the finely chopped garlic, chilli, sea salt and black pepper.

Scatter the sliced mint over the zucchini, and finally sprinkle the dish with the vinegar. Serve at room temperature.

If serving the next day, cover the plate with clingfilm and keep in a cool place, not the refrigerator.

Caponata

CAPONATA

There are as many ways to make caponata as there are cooks in Sicily. The basis of caponata is the popular aubergine, and the dish evolves according to what other vegetables you wish to include. All caponatas have wine vinegar as part of the seasoning and most include capers, olives and pine nuts. This recipe has celery as its other strong flavour, which makes a light, refreshing version.

For 6

1 large round, pale aubergine, about 12cm in diameter, or 2 medium round, pale aubergines

sea salt and freshly ground black pepper

2 whole heads of celery, with leaves

1 large red onion, peeled

2 ripe plum tomatoes, or 3 drained from a tin

extra virgin olive oil

1 garlic clove, peeled and finely sliced

2 dried red chillies, crumbled

3 tablespoons black Ligurian olives, stoned and kept whole

2 tablespoons pine nuts

2 tablespoons salted capers, rinsed, then soaked in 2 tablespoons red wine vinegar

3 tablespoons mint leaves, washed

6 slices of sourdough bread

Cut the aubergine into 1.5cm cubes and place in a colander. Sprinkle with sea salt and drain for 30 minutes. Wash off the salt and pat dry.

Cut the tender white part of the celery into 2cm lengths. Put them into a pan, cover with water, add 1 teaspoon of sea salt and bring to the boil. Cook for 3 minutes, then drain. Cut the onion into fine slices and peel and core the tomatoes, then chop them into 1cm pieces.

Heat 3–4 tablespoons of olive oil in a frying pan, and add the aubergine pieces in batches so that they just cover the bottom of the pan. Fry over a medium high heat for about 5 minutes, turning the pieces over until brown on all sides. Remove and drain on kitchen paper. Repeat this process; you may need to use extra olive oil if it has all been absorbed in the first batch.

Wipe the pan clean and return it to the heat. Add 2 tablespoons of olive oil and the onion. Reduce the heat and gently soften the onion until it becomes golden; this will take 10 minutes. Add the garlic and celery, and continue to cook for a further 5 minutes, to combine the flavours. Season with pepper and crumble in the chillies. Add the tomato pieces and just let them warm up in the mixture, but not really cook, then stir in the aubergines. Cook all the vegetables together briefly for 5 minutes. Test for seasoning and stir in the olives, pine nuts and the capers including the vinegar they have been soaking in. Finally, chop the mint and stir it into the mixture with a drizzle of sweet extra virgin olive oil.

Toast the bread on both sides to make bruschetta, and serve with the caponata.

PEPERONATA

STEWED PEPPERS

This is a simple way of cooking peppers slowly in a pan with onions. The interesting part of this recipe is adding the uncooked tomatoes at the end.

For 8–10

8 red peppers

4 ripe plum tomatoes

3 tablespoons extra virgin olive oil

3 red onions, peeled and finely sliced

2 garlic cloves, peeled and finely sliced

sea salt and freshly ground black pepper

Cut the peppers into long slices about 2cm wide, removing the seeds, membrane and core.

Plunge the tomatoes into boiling water for a few minutes. Remove and, when cool enough to handle, slip off the skins, cut in half, and squeeze out the seeds and juice. Chop coarsely.

In a large, thick-bottomed frying pan, heat the olive oil. Add the onions, garlic and peppers, stir to coat them in the oil, and lower the heat. Season well and cook for about an hour, uncovered, until the peppers are very soft but not brown.

Raise the heat, remove the lid, and add the tomatoes. Cook for a further 10 minutes, check the seasoning, and serve.

FAGIOLINI CON PREZZEMOLO

GREEN BEANS WITH PARSLEY AND VINEGAR

When you pick green beans from the garden, or buy fresh, recently picked beans in the local market, the flavour is so pronounced that it lasts through the long cooking and the soft texture of the beans absorbs the oil and herbs. Green beans cooked this way wrap around the fork like spaghetti.

For 4–6

sea salt and freshly ground black pepper
1kg green beans, trimmed
3 tablespoons roughly chopped fresh flat-leaf parsley
2 garlic cloves, peeled and finely chopped
2 tablespoons red wine vinegar
5 tablespoons extra virgin olive oil

Boil an abundant amount of water in a pan with a little sea salt. Add the green beans and cook for 15 minutes. Drain, leave to cool a bit, then combine with the parsley, garlic, vinegar and olive oil. Season well.

Stewed peppers, green beans with parsley and vinegar

INSALATA DI OVOLI

OVOLI SALAD

Late summer and early autumn brings ovoli, which were Julius Caesar's favourite. They are gathered in the chestnut and oak woods at the foothills of the Apennines. Amanita caesarea, 'Caesar's mushroom', is a beautiful orange-capped variety of fungi, oval in shape, the size of a chicken's egg. Ovoli are picked very young, before the cap opens, when the texture is still firm. As the cap opens up the mushroom becomes very fragile and loses its flavour.

Ovoli are almost always eaten raw, finely sliced, drizzled with lemon juice and extra virgin olive oil. Often shavings of Parmesan are mixed in. In Florence in the Osteria Ruggerio they also mix rocket leaves into this most exceptional mushroom salad.

For 2–4, depending on size of ovoli

3 ovoli mushrooms

sea salt and freshly ground black pepper

50g Parmesan shavings

extra virgin olive oil

1 lemon, quartered

Peel off the white skin of the ovoli and clean the tops of the caps with a damp cloth. Keep the stem, but trim off the earthy bits from the bulbous base.

Using a small, very sharp knife, finely slice through the caps and stems. Lay the slices over each plate and season with sea salt and black pepper. Lay the Parmesan shavings over so that they partially cover the ovoli, drizzle with olive oil and serve with a wedge of lemon.

PORCINI ARROSTO

ROAST WHOLE FRESH PORCINI

Fresh porcini mushrooms are probably the most sought-after mushrooms for cooking, particularly in Italy, where you will find beautiful displays in the markets from late August through to the end of October, or until the first frost.

The porcini mushrooms are often sorted into varying qualities; the top quality and most expensive are the fresh, whole, large, deep-coloured caps with their stalks intact. They are firm to touch and have a strong perfume. These are the ones you should choose for this recipe. The smaller ones, which may be partially broken, are used for pasta or polenta sauces and will be considerably cheaper. Avoid porcini that are very soft, as they will have lost their flavour and will become slimy when cooked.

Porcini grow all over the UK, and finding and picking them yourself is one of the greatest pleasures.

For 4

1kg whole fresh firm porcini mushrooms

3 tablespoons extra virgin olive oil

sea salt and freshly ground black pepper

3 garlic cloves, peeled and cut into eighths

1 tablespoon fresh thyme leaves

120ml white wine

To prepare the fresh porcini mushrooms, use a damp cloth and wipe the caps clean, keeping the spongy underside dry. Use a small knife to scrape the stems and cut off any soft or earthy bits.

Preheat the oven to 220°C. Choose a large thick-bottomed pan or casserole dish with an ovenproof handle that will fit in your oven. Heat the pan with the olive oil in it until very hot, almost smoking. Add the whole mushrooms and scatter over a little salt. Turn the mushrooms over in the hot oil to lightly brown – this takes seconds – then add the garlic, thyme leaves and a scattering of pepper. Remove from the heat, add the wine, and place the pan in the oven, uncovered, for 10–15 minutes, turning the mushrooms over after 5 minutes, checking they are moist and tender.

Serve with grilled or roasted meats.

ZUCCA AI FERRI

GRILLED PUMPKIN

We were introduced to this recipe in the kitchens of Agriturismo La Tenuta Seliano, south of Naples, located in a lovely eighteenth-century villa surrounded by gardens, the owners of which have beautiful herds of black buffalo and make some of the most delicious mozzarella.

For dinner one night, we were greeted with plates of grilled marinated pumpkin with their creamy mozzarella. The combination was so completely right that we always put these two ingredients together during the pumpkin and squash season.

For 6–8

1 large, ripe pumpkin or orange squash with firm, sweet flesh, e.g. peanut, onion or butternut

sea salt and freshly ground black pepper

1 dried red chilli (optional)

extra virgin olive oil

2 teaspoons dried oregano or 3 tablespoons fresh marjoram

juice of 1 large lemon

Peel the pumpkin whole; we use a Y-shaped potato peeler, although you may find it easier to use a sharp knife as the skin of some squash is hard. Cut the pumpkin in half across; if using butternut or peanut squash, cut across where the bulge starts dividing it between the part with no seeds and the bulbous part containing the seeds.

Slice the pumpkin into fine discs, 5mm thick. You should be able to get about 30 slices. Where there are seeds, scrape them out, using the edge of a dessertspoon, before slicing.

Bring a large pan of salted water to the boil. Add the discs and rings in batches and cook for 1 minute. Do not overcook or the slices will fall apart. Drain on kitchen paper, and pat dry.

Preheat a griddle pan. When it's hot, lay on the pieces of squash and grill briefly for about a minute; they cook very quickly. Turn and grill on the other side, until charred and just soft.

When you have finished grilling, lay the pieces of squash on a large serving plate and, while still warm, scatter over sea salt, black pepper, and dried chilli if you like it spicy. Then drizzle over 3 tablespoons of olive oil. Finally, scatter over the dried oregano or fresh marjoram.

To serve, squeeze over lemon juice, then gather the slices together into a small pile on each plate.

The pumpkins you find in southern Italy usually taste richer and are a darker colour than the common butternut found here

PINZIMONIO CON OLIO NUOVO

ITALIAN RAW VEGETABLES WITH NEW SEASON'S EXTRA VIRGIN OLIVE OIL

This Roman dish is more of a suggestion than a recipe. Place a large plate with an assortment of the freshest seasonal vegetables on the table, give everybody a small bowl, into which you pour the best flavoured new season's olive oil, and make sure there is plenty of sea salt on the table.

Pinzimonio is a dish often offered to us when, as a group, we visit the olive oil producers in November, when they have started their production of olive oil. If you are in Tuscany at this time, you will have the chance to try this dish in many of the small trattorias. It is a great way of showing off an exceptional olive oil, and a colourful talking point to start off a meal. The vegetables usually found in Italy at that time of year are the new season's artichokes, Florence fennel bulbs, carrots and celery hearts. Raw artichokes have a delicious flavour when young and just picked. There are many varieties, but sweetest of all are the Violetta di Chioggia, which are purple-leaved with yellowish hearts and are easy to peel.

For 6

6 small violetta artichokes, sold with their stems intact

1 lemon

3 fennel bulbs

2 heads of leafy celery, washed

6 small carrots

250ml extra virgin olive oil

sea salt

Peel just a few of the tough outer leaves from the artichoke hearts, keeping the stems and a few of the leaves attached. Cut each artichoke in half downwards through the stalk. Squeeze a little lemon juice on to the cut side if you are not going to serve the pinzimonio straight away.

Remove the tough outer leaves of the fennel bulbs and cut each bulb in half and then into quarters. Pull off the green outer stalks from the celery heads and cut off the tops. Cut in half lengthways and then cut each heart lengthways into three. Peel the carrots and leave them whole.

Pile the vegetables on to a serving plate and serve individual small bowls of olive oil. Let everybody help themselves to a selection of the vegetables and suggest that each vegetable is dipped into the oil before eating. Sprinkle the salt on as you go.

Fresh borlotti have a unique creamy consistency and a delicious nutty flavour, so it is not surprising that we look forward to the moment when they first arrive from Italy

BORLOTTI CON PORCINI

FRESH BORLOTTI WITH RAW PORCINI

There is a brief moment as summer overlaps with autumn when fresh borlotti beans are still available, the fresh porcini mushrooms are beginning to appear, and the tomatoes are sweet and ripe. This recipe is an adaptation of one eaten in the restaurant U Gianci in Liguria. It is very simple to put together, but relies on the perfection of each ingredient.

For 12

350g fresh borlotti beans, in their pods

2 garlic cloves, peeled

1 bunch of fresh sage

3 fresh ripe plum tomatoes

extra virgin olive oil

sea salt

250g fresh porcini mushrooms

Pod the beans and place in a small pan. Cover with water and add 1 garlic clove, the sage and 1 whole tomato. Add 2 tablespoons of olive oil and cover. Bring to the boil and reduce the heat to a simmer. Cook for 30 minutes, or until the beans are tender. Drain off most of the liquid and discard the sage. Mash the garlic and tomato into the beans, discarding the tomato skin, and season with sea salt. Keep warm.

Wipe the mushrooms with a damp cloth, keeping them whole, and cut them into roughly 2cm thick slices through the cap and stem. Finely slice the remaining garlic clove. Pierce the skins of the rest of the tomatoes with a sharp knife, then place in a bowl and pour over boiling water to cover. Remove after 30 seconds and immediately slip off the skins. Chop the tomatoes into a rough pulp, pushing away and discarding excess seeds and juice.

Heat 3 tablespoons of olive oil in a medium frying pan. When hot, add the mushrooms. As they begin to brown, add the garlic and stir to turn the slices over. This will take just a few minutes. While still very hot, add the tomato pieces and, using a slotted spoon, the borlotti beans. You may not need to use all the beans, as the balance of beans to mushrooms should be about 50:50. Stir just briefly to combine and season. Serve on bruschetta or with grilled meat. Keep any remaining borlotti in their juice, covered, in the refrigerator.

Cannellini

Chickpeas with rosemary and garlic

TREVISANO TARDIVO

BRAISED RADICCHIO DI TREVISO

From late November to early January, tardivo, a variety of radicchio, is in season. It has dark red, spear-shaped leaves, curved at the tips, with creamy white spines attached to a thick root, the centre of which is the edible part. Grown in Treviso in a very particular way, the plants are forced in the dark with their roots in warm water to develop crisp winter leaves which have the most delicious bittersweet flavour. The leaves alone make a different winter salad, dressed either with olive oil and white wine vinegar with plenty of salt, or with balsamic vinegar and lemon.

In the restaurants around the cities of Treviso and Venice, you always see grilled or braised tardivo on the menu. In this recipe the heads are divided lengthwise into quarters, the root peeled down to the tender pure white part, and braised. We cook tardivo this way at the River Café.

For 6

3 heads of radicchio di Treviso tardivo (weighing about 500g)

extra virgin olive oil

sea salt and freshly ground black pepper

2 tablespoons fresh thyme leaves

150ml white wine, such as Soave Classico

To prepare the radicchio, pull off and discard any withered outer leaves, or leaves that have a green tinge; you are then left with the firm, crisp hearts. Use a potato peeler or small sharp knife to peel the root down to the tender pure white part. Cut off the deep coloured tips, about 4cm from the top, and set aside.

Cut the hearts in half lengthwise through the stalk then cut each half lengthwise again into quarters. If the hearts are really big, cut each half into thirds.

Use a large, flat, thick-bottomed frying pan to heat 2 tablespoons of olive oil until almost smoking. Add the pieces of radicchio in one layer, scatter over the salt and thyme leaves, and cook for about 2 minutes, just to lightly brown. Turn the pieces over, add the wine, and let it bubble and reduce; this will take a few minutes. Then add the reserved tips, toss together, and test for seasoning. Drizzle a little extra virgin olive oil over and serve warm.

WINTER LEAF SALAD

The mixture of winter salad in the picture is a choice of salad leaves rarely found outside Italy. In fact, this particular mixture is a selection from the Milan market that we are lucky enough to be able to buy for the River Café.

In the top left-hand corner of the box are cicorino grumulo verde and rosso. This is a variety of chicory which grows in small rosettes, has a bittersweet taste and a firm texture. It does grow in the UK but few people seem to know about it. In Italy, it is usually mixed with other leaves. Longino is a long-leafed mâche or corn salad, which is below the grumulo. It has fleshy ends, and is sweet in flavour. There are two varieties of mâche leaves. The other one is songrino, in the top right-hand corner, which has little round deep green leaves and is slightly furry, with a strong earthy taste, more like a wild salad. The yellow leaf dandelion is French, a crisp bitter leaf salad. The Italian dandelion tarrassaco is a cultivated leaf that, when small, is used in salads and, when larger, is cooked like spinach. The taste is also quite bitter.

Below the tarrassaco is a bunch of young chicory leaves: cicoria in mazzetto. They are always sold in these bunches and, because they are the inner tender leaves of the chicory plant, they have a sweet taste not unlike lettuce. Below the cicoria in mazzetto is a bunch of what is known as domestic rocket, Rucola domestica, or large-leaf rocket. This leaf has a good strong texture and is vital in a mixed leaf salad, contributing a peppery flavour. The yellow and red speckled Castelfranco is a relative of radicchio that has been cultivated especially for salads. It is a colourful part of a winter salad, with a mild bitter taste.

The dark green Italian watercress is not unlike the larger-leaf variety that grows in the UK. Its flavour is very strong and the leaves are quite fleshy. It is a deliciously different flavour to complement the bitter leaves.

These leaves are best dressed with a good red wine vinegar, sea salt, black pepper and extra virgin olive oil. We usually mix one quarter vinegar to three quarters olive oil.

tarrassaco

Coop.Saccagnana

songrino

cicorino grumulo verde

cicorino grumulo rosso

yellow leaf dandelion

cicoria in mazzetto

longino

Italian watercress

Castelfranco

Rucola domestica

FINOCCHIO TRIFOLATI

BRAISED FENNEL

The method of braising vegetables in olive oil and then cooking them slowly with the addition of water is particularly Italian. The fibrous fennel bulb is ideal for long cooking, and allows the sweet delicate flavour to develop as the water and olive oil are absorbed.

For 6
4 large fennel bulbs
3 tablespoons extra virgin olive oil
3 garlic cloves, peeled
sea salt and freshly ground black pepper

Cut off and discard the fennel tops. Trim away the outer layers of the fennel bulb and slice the bulb lengthways into quarters or eighths, depending on the size of the bulb.

In a large frying pan or pan, heat the olive oil. Add the fennel and garlic and toss over a medium heat for 5 minutes. Season with salt and pepper. When the fennel is beginning to colour, reduce the heat and cook gently for a further 15 minutes or so.

Add enough boiling water just to cover the fennel and continue cooking over a low heat until it is soft enough to pierce with a fork and the water is totally absorbed. By the time it is ready – about 25 minutes – the fennel should be a pale brown colour.

SORBETS & ICE CREAMS

SORBETS & ICE CREAMS

Enter a gelateria in Italy and the choice of sorbet and ice cream flavours is dazzling: rich ice creams made with vin santo or marsala, traditional Italian dessert flavours such as zuppa inglese or tiramisù, or those made with the purest, freshest seasonal fruit. In every city, town or village you will see people old and young walking down the street or sitting on benches eating ice cream. When we arrive anywhere in Italy, just as we search out the best markets and the best restaurants, we also search out the best gelateria.

Gelaterias are meeting places, not only to eat ice cream but to enjoy an espresso or an aperitivo after work, before a football game, or simply as a place to stop and chat while taking the time-honoured passeggiata at sunset. They are often family-run – look for the sign 'produzione propria', which declares they make the ice creams on the premises. The people who work there are proud of their ice cream, urging you to taste the varieties with small coloured plastic spoons.

Years ago, when we were filming in Florence, we were advised to visit a particular gelateria as they made an extraordinary marmalade ice cream. This was unlike any other traditional gelateria we had been to; we found the owner in his kitchen experimenting with subtle, modern flavours – an extra bitter chocolate sorbet, a granita of pear and lemon, and a pistachio ice cream that was slightly grainy rather than smooth. We went back to the River Café and developed these recipes and they are here in this book.

The ice creams we make most often are those we most associate with Italy – vanilla, hazelnut, pistachio, caramel, chocolate chip – and, like everything we cook, we aim for a taste that is strong and assertive, defining the quality of the ingredients. When making an ice cream such as caramel, we take the sugar and water to the stage where it is almost black; we roast hazelnuts to a dark colour and then grind and press them through a sieve to get every bit of flavour out of them. Our chocolate sorbet is extra bitter as we use two different kinds of bittersweet chocolate together with a 100% cocoa powder.

What we think truly identifies our sorbets is that their flavour bursts in your mouth. It is absolutely essential that you make them with nothing other than beautiful, ripe fruit in season. This is what we do: when we have delicious chestnuts, we make a chestnut and brandy sorbet, and if we have great pears we'll make a granita. The white peach Bellini granita in this chapter works fabulously, and that came from just turning the Bellini cocktail into a sorbet. When we make sorbets at home we freeze them in shallow trays rather than churn them in an ice cream machine.

SORBETTO DI RIBES

BLACKCURRANT SORBET

For 6–8

1kg ripe blackcurrants, washed and stalks removed
500g caster sugar

Put the blackcurrants and sugar into a medium pan over a low heat. Stir until the currants are just bursting, about 5 minutes, and remove from the heat immediately. It is crucial when making this recipe that you do not 'cook' the blackcurrants, but take them off the heat the moment they start to burst open. Push them through a sieve into a bowl, using a wooden spoon or ladle.

Pour this juice into an ice cream machine and churn until frozen, or freeze in flat trays in your freezer, mashing the sorbet with a fork every 10–15 minutes to break up the crystals until it is solid and of a creamy consistency. Scrape the sorbet into a deeper smaller container to store until you are ready to serve it.

Wash the blackcurrants before cooking, so that there is a bit of water clinging to them when you put them into the pan with the sugar

SORBETTO DI CASTAGNA

CHESTNUT AND BRANDY SORBET

This is a very festive and unusual sorbet to make when the chestnuts are fresh. It is delicious served alongside our extra bitter chocolate sorbet (see page 334).When buying chestnuts, always choose those with a rounded shape and glossy outer skin, which indicates their freshness. Chestnuts dry out and lose their flavour very quickly; don't use these for sorbet.

For 8

1.5kg fresh whole chestnuts
2 vanilla pods
1.5 litres water
500g sugar
200ml Vecchia Romagna brandy

Score each chestnut on the rounded side, using a small sharp knife. Place in a small pan and cover with cold water. Bring the water to the boil for 1 minute, then remove from the heat. As soon as the chestnuts are cool enough to touch – they must not be cold, otherwise the skin will not come off – take them out of the water one by one and peel off the outer and inner skins. Keep the water warm – with this quantity of chestnuts to peel you may have to return the pan to the heat. Discard any discoloured bits and crumble the chestnuts into small pieces.

Split the vanilla pods lengthwise. Put them into a large thick-bottomed pan with the water and sugar and bring to the boil. Cook on a high heat for 5 minutes, until reduced to a light syrup. Add the chestnuts and simmer gently for 10–15 minutes, then strain, keeping the syrup in a jug, and put the chestnuts back into the pan. Remove the vanilla pods from the syrup, use a teaspoon to scrape the seeds into the chestnuts, and discard the pods. Purée the chestnuts with a potato masher in the pan, or transfer to a food processor, then loosen the purée by stirring all the strained syrup back into it. Add the brandy and mix well. Test for sweetness and leave to cool completely.

Either put the mixture into an ice cream machine and churn until frozen, in batches if necessary, or pour into flat freezer trays and freeze until solid. Stir with a fork to break up the crystals every half hour until you have a creamy consistency.

SORBETTO DI CIOCCOLATA

EXTRA BITTER CHOCOLATE SORBET

Often, gelaterias offer a range of chocolate sorbets and ice creams. These vary in darkness and strength of chocolate flavour. We always go for the darkest on offer, and came up with this recipe to satisfy our after-dinner cravings — it's ideal if you're feeling full, as it's very light.

For 4–6

2 vanilla pods

500ml semi-skimmed milk

200ml water

120g light brown sugar

250g dark chocolate, 75% or 85% cocoa solids

50g cocoa powder, 100%

Split the vanilla pods in half lengthwise. Put the milk, water, sugar and vanilla pods into a small thick-bottomed pan and slowly bring to the boil, then take off the heat. Remove the vanilla pods from the pan, use a teaspoon to scrape the seeds back into the milk, and discard the pods.

Chop the chocolate into small pieces and add to the milk. Stir to allow the chocolate to completely melt into the mixture. Put the pan back on a low heat and stir in the cocoa powder until completely dissolved. Leave to cool.

Pour the mixture into an ice cream machine and churn until frozen, or freeze in a flat tray, stirring at intervals with a fork to break up any crystals that may form during the freezing process.

THREE CHOCOLATE ICE CREAM

We use three different kinds of chocolate to make this ice cream more interesting: 75% or 85% cocoa solid chocolate with a fruity flavour is ideal for the chips, while a 100% bitter chocolate and a 70% work for the chocolate base.

For 8–10

8 large free-range organic egg yolks

200g caster sugar

700ml full-fat milk

500ml double cream

200g bitter chocolate, 100% cocoa solids

200g chocolate, 70% cocoa solids

100g chocolate, 75% or 85% cocoa solids, roughly chopped into 0.5cm pieces or smaller

In an electric mixer, beat the egg yolks and sugar for about 5 minutes, until they have doubled in size and are thick and pale in colour.

In a medium thick-bottomed pan, heat the milk and cream to just below boiling point. Slowly pour this mixture into the eggs and sugar, beating very slowly. Pour back into the pan and cook very gently over a low heat, stirring until the custard mixture is thick enough to coat the back of a spoon; this will take 10–15 minutes. Remove from the heat, pour into a bowl and leave to cool.

Melt the 100% and 70% chocolates in a bowl over simmering water and stir into the custard. Stir thoroughly to combine, and leave to cool.

Put the mixture into an ice cream machine and churn until half frozen. Add the chocolate chips and stir to combine, then churn until frozen — you may have to do this in batches. Alternatively, freeze in a shallow tray, adding the chocolate chips halfway through, scraping the mixture with a fork every 15 minutes as it freezes until you have a creamy frozen consistency. Remove from the tray to a deeper container for storing until you want to serve it.

GELATO AL MARSALA

MARSALA ICE CREAM

Marsala Vergine is the purest of the dry Sicilian dessert wines, gold in colour with the subtle flavour of almonds and honey. It is perfect for making this delicious ice cream.

For 8–10

10 large free-range organic egg yolks
200g caster sugar
350ml dry white Marsala (Marsala Vergine is best)
450ml double cream

In an electric mixer, beat the egg yolks and sugar together until they are light and creamy and have trebled in volume.

Half fill a large pan with water and bring to the boil, then turn the heat down so that the water is gently simmering. Pour the egg yolk mixture into a bowl that will sit comfortably over the pan but not touch the water. Whisk continuously for 10 minutes, then add half the Marsala and continue to whisk and cook until this custard mixture thickens so that it coats the back of a spoon and has almost reached boiling point; this will take about 10–15 minutes. Remove from the heat and cool.

Lightly whip the cream and fold it into the custard. Stir in the remaining Marsala and leave to cool.

Pour the mixture into an ice cream machine and churn — in batches if necessary — until just beginning to freeze, then place in the freezer to become firm and frozen.

GRANITA DI PERE

PEAR AND LEMON GRANITA

The fresh, fruity flavour of this granita will be achieved if you use either Comice, a very tender, aromatic, richly flavoured pear with creamy white flesh, or Conference, which has a thick skin and a sweet flavour. Conference pears are widely available and are usually less expensive than Comice. They are easily recognized by their elongated shape. Do not use William pears for granita – their firm grainy texture and sweetness make them better for cooking.

For 6–8

5 very ripe pears

150g caster sugar

juice of 1 large lemon

Peel, core and roughly chop the pears, then mash with a fork. The pears should not be smooth, but should retain a bit of texture. Add the sugar and lemon juice and mix well.

Pour into shallow ice trays or cake tins and put into the freezer. Allow the juice to freeze partially, for about 20–30 minutes. Mash with a fork to break up the ice crystals, then return to the freezer and leave for a further 20 minutes. Repeat this process, mashing up the frozen juice, returning it to the freezer and freezing, until you have a hard, dry, crystalline granita. This will take up to 2½ hours.

BELLINI

This recipe for Bellini has evolved over the years at the River Café, always using the Harry's Bar Bellini as the benchmark. Last summer in early July in Venice, as the first white peaches were appearing, the Bellinis were a beautiful cherry blossom pink and as delicious as we have ever had. We always ask the barman for hints on how to achieve the right colour and fruitiness, and he gave us this new version. The pinkness of the Bellini comes from the dark red colour beneath the peach skin. So choose white peaches with deep red skins, and make sure they are ripe and juicy.

For 6

6 very ripe white peaches

1–2 lemons, halved

3 tablespoons caster sugar

1 bottle of prosecco, refrigerated

Bring a large pan of water to the boil. Have ready a large bowl of cold water with 2 tumblers of ice cubes in it. Place a few of the peaches at a time in the boiling water and after just a few seconds remove them with a slotted spoon and immediately put them into the iced water. Do this in batches so that the peaches are completely submerged, and do not let them cook.

When cool enough to handle, slip off most of the peach skin with your hands, leaving a little, as this improves the colour of the Bellini. Rub each peeled peach all over with half a lemon; this also helps to keep the colour. Tear the peaches up into small pieces, working over a bowl so that you can collect the juice and pulp as you do so. Then rub your hands with lemon juice and use them to mash the pulp into the juice. Do all this as quickly as you can, to prevent the peaches from oxidizing and going brown. Now add the sugar and taste for sweetness, adding the remaining half lemon if necessary. Cover the peach pulp with clingfilm, making sure it touches the surface, which will stop any further oxidization. Put into the fridge to cool. Alternatively, pulp the skinned peaches in a juicer or food processor, then cover and leave to cool.

When you are ready to serve your Bellinis, blend the pulp in a juicer or food processor until smooth, if you have not already done so. Test for sweetness, adding more sugar or lemon if necessary. Use champagne flutes or small tumblers: fill one third with peach pulp and top up very slowly with cold prosecco, adding more as the froth subsides.

GRANITA BELLINI

Every summer, Italian ice cream makers come up with wonderful new flavours. This granita came from our kitchen, where we enjoy experimenting with flavours. It was inspired by the white peach cocktail (see page 347) that we make when the peaches are in season.

For 6–8

6 ripe white peaches (to yield 750ml peach pulp, see below)

2 large lemons

160g caster sugar

500ml prosecco

To make the peach pulp, bring a large pan of water to the boil. Have ready a large bowl filled with cold water and about 250g of ice cubes. Drop the peaches 2 at a time into the boiling water and leave for 1 minute. Remove with a slotted spoon and place in the iced water.

Have ready a second bowl; slip off the skins from the peaches with your hands and break the peach flesh away from the stone into the bowl. Do this over the bowl to collect all the juice, squeezing the juice of ½ a lemon over to prevent the peaches oxidizing, i.e. going brown. Add 1 teaspoon of sugar to the pulp.

Place the pulp in a blender and purée until smooth. Test for sweetness, adding more sugar or lemon juice according to the ripeness of the peaches.

To make the granita, put the rest of the sugar into a small pan with 150ml of water and whisk over a low heat until the sugar is completely dissolved. Boil to reduce by half, and allow to cool. Add a quarter of the peach purée and stir gently, then stir in the remainder.

Now add the juice of 1 lemon and finally pour in the prosecco. Mix together and taste for sweetness. Add more lemon or sugar if necessary. Pour into a flat tray and freeze to a slushy consistency, stirring every 15 minutes with a fork. Serve in bowls or glasses previously cooled in the fridge.

CAKES

CAKES

Pasticcerie – cakes, tarts and biscuits – are an important part of everyday life in Italy. A Milanese friend, Filippo Petteni, describes going out on a Friday night with his friends when he was a teenager, going back to any one of their homes in the early hours of the morning, and waking up to a delicious crostata – jam tart – on the kitchen table made by the grandmother of the house; a way of saying, 'I am here to take care of you.' Talk to an Italian from any region and they will tell you of the Sunday morning ritual of going to church, then stopping at a pasticceria to buy cakes and pastries to take home. Or they might describe how Italians take cakes rather than flowers when visiting friends; arranged on delicate paper trays, they are always beautifully wrapped in lovely coloured tissue paper and tied with ribbon.

Cakes in Italy basically fall into two categories: the elaborate desserts of the pasticceria and the simpler cakes made at home. Though Italians do not tend to think of desserts as the grand finale to a meal, there are some that are celebratory and indulgent, such as the dramatic Monte Bianco, a mountain of cream covered with puréed chestnuts, and the popular pannacotta from Piedmont.

Go to a café in Milan and you will see the most elegant people having afternoon coffee and eating millefeuille. In Sicily, the coffee bars have endless trays of brightly coloured marzipan-covered pastries and ricotta-stuffed cakes. In Florence, try the classic torta della nonna in as many places as you can; the Bar Gilli in the Piazza Republica makes our favourite version. Torta di Capri is just as its name implies – a cake made on the isle of Capri. Around the square at the top of the island you will see everyone eating this dark, bitter chocolate cake. As it is so rich it is served in small pieces. The chocolate and almonds are roughly ground together, giving it a unique texture.

Panettone is a traditional Milanese cake usually prepared for the holidays of Christmas and New Year. Its origin dates back to the Roman Empire, when leavened bread was sweetened with honey. While is not hard to make, it does require time, as the dough needs to rise several times. Panettone is traditionally made with candied citrus fruit, raisins, and a large amount of butter, and some also include chocolate.

We were taught to make strudel by Dada Rogers, who lived in Trieste – once part of the Austro-Hungarian Empire, where strudel-making is a tradition. Its thin dough can be used to wrap various juicy seasonal fruits and berries.

The cakes made at home are to be eaten at any time of day, rather than something dramatic to serve at the end of the meal. They are often frugal, using only the local ingredients: for example, polenta, chestnut flour, hazelnuts and ricotta in the north, and liquor, almonds, pine nuts and raisins in the south. Most cooks make crostatas at home because they make their own jam; in this chapter we have included the recipe for a mixed fruit jam we made in Tuscany – and it is perfect in a crostata.

It is often said that Italians have their cakes at breakfast, their ice cream while walking down the street, and their espresso at the end of the meal. We have included recipes for cantuccini, riciarelli and Florentines for the times you want to have a coffee or vin santo and savour something sweet.

CROSTATA DI MARMELLATA

JAM TART

This delicious tart can also be made with the mixed summer fruit jam or the peach and rosemary jam on pages 356 and 359.

For 10
For the pastry
350g plain flour
175g unsalted butter
100g icing sugar, plus extra for dusting
3 large free-range organic egg yolks

For the jam
2kg quinces, washed, cored and quartered
juice of 2 large oranges
preserving sugar

For the pastry, pulse the flour and butter in a food processor until the mixture resembles coarse breadcrumbs. Add the sugar, then the egg yolks, and pulse again. The mixture will immediately combine and leave the sides of the bowl. Remove, wrap in clingfilm and chill for at least an hour. Preheat the oven to 160°C. Coarsely grate two-thirds of the pastry into a 30cm loose-bottomed fluted fan tin and press it evenly on to the sides and the base. Bake blind for 20 minutes, until very light brown. Leave to cool.

For the jam, gently heat the quince pieces in a thick-bottomed pan with the orange juice. Cook slowly until the quinces become soft and darker, adding more orange juice if they start to catch on the bottom of the pan. Stir while they are cooking to break up the pieces of fruit. This will take up to 30 minutes. Weigh the pulp and measure out two-thirds of its weight in preserving sugar. Add the sugar to the pulp and return it to the pan. Cook until the mixture has become thick and shiny and leaves the sides of the pan, about 15 minutes. The jam should set when cooled at this stage.

Spread a 1cm thick layer of set jam over the base of the tart shell. You will need about 1kg of jam; store the rest in sterilized jars (see page 356). Roll out the remaining pastry and cut into long strips. Cover the jam with the strips in a criss-cross pattern and bake for 25 minutes, or until the pastry is lightly brown. Remove from the oven, leave to cool, and finish with a dusting of icing sugar.

MARMELLATA ESTIVA

MIXED SUMMER FRUIT JAM

When we asked one of our Italian friends, who loves to cook for us in the summer, for this recipe for a summer jam, she was so vague about the ingredients and method that we asked her to make it again so we could watch. Another friend, who lives in the Maremma, said he had made a jam of peaches and rosemary which was delicious with ice cream (see page 359).

Makes about 5kg

1 small cantaloupe melon, peeled, deseeded and cut into pieces

1kg peaches, stoned and cut into pieces

1kg plums, stoned and cut into pieces

500g black grapes

500g apples, peeled and cored, cut into pieces

1 bottle of white wine

3kg caster sugar

The total weight of the fruit before preparation should be approximately 4kg.

Put the prepared fruit into a very large ovenproof pan with the wine. Bring to the boil, then lower the heat to a gentle simmer. Cook for 1–1½ hours. A lot of liquid will come out of the fruit, and this will reduce down to a rich compote. Add the sugar and stir until it has dissolved. Continue cooking for another 2 hours.

Preheat the oven to 250°C. Place the pan in the oven and cook, stirring occasionally, for 1 hour. Remove, leave to cool, then put into sterilized jars (see below) or use to make a crostata (see page 354).

To sterilize your jars, first wash them in hot soapy water and rinse thoroughly, then dry them out for 10 minutes in the oven at 100°C. Alternatively run them through a hot cycle on the dishwasher. Make sure the jars are hot when you pour in the jam, otherwise they may crack.

The ingredients depend on what fruit you have
to combine with the basics of melon, peaches and plums

TORTA DI POLENTA

ALMOND, RICOTTA AND POLENTA CAKE

For years we have been making a polenta and almond cake, serving it with blood oranges in the winter for a dessert or putting it on the bar to eat at any time of the day with an espresso or cappuccino. Adding ricotta transforms it into a lighter and creamier cake.

For 10–12; makes 1 x 26cm cake

225g unsalted butter, softened, plus a little for the tin

250g blanched almonds

100g polenta flour

finely grated zest of 6 lemons

250g caster sugar

6 large free-range organic eggs, separated

300g fresh ricotta cheese

juice of 3 lemons

Preheat the oven to 150°C. Butter a 26cm round cake tin and line it with greaseproof paper.

Coarsely chop the almonds in a food processor. Combine with the polenta flour and lemon zest. Beat the butter and sugar together using an electric mixer until pale and light. Add the egg yolks one by one, then add the almond mixture and fold together.

Put the ricotta into a bowl and beat lightly with a fork. Add the lemon juice. In another bowl, whisk the egg whites until they form soft peaks. Fold the egg whites into the almond mixture and finally stir in the ricotta.

Spoon the mixture into the prepared tin and bake in the oven for 40–50 minutes, until set. Test by inserting a skewer, which should come out clean. Leave in the tin to cool for 10 minutes before turning out.

Torta della nonna

STRUDEL

BLACKBERRY AND APPLE STRUDEL

For 8–10

For the dough

225g bread flour, sifted

2 teaspoons caster sugar

1 teaspoon melted unsalted butter, plus 2 tablespoons

1 medium free-range organic egg, beaten

For the filling

1kg apples, peeled, cored and cut into 2cm pieces

150g caster sugar

125 dried breadcrumbs

150g blackberries

100g melted unsalted butter

Put the flour into a large bowl. Make a well in the centre and add the sugar, 1 teaspoon of melted butter and the egg. Add enough water to make a sticky dough and knead for about 10 minutes, until the dough is no longer sticky but has a silky sheen. Brush lightly with the 2 tablespoons of melted butter and leave to rest for half an hour. Put the apples into a bowl and toss with the sugar and half the breadcrumbs. Add the blackberries and toss.

Preheat the oven to 200°C. An easy way to roll out the strudel dough is to do so on a floured cloth or large tea towel, otherwise just generously flour your worktop or table. Roll out the dough from the centre until it is thin. Place the backs of your hands under the dough and carefully lift and stretch and pull it from all sides until it is as thin as tissue paper and almost transparent. You should have a sheet of dough measuring approximately 50 x 80cm. Trim off the edges.

Brush the sheet of dough with some of the melted butter, and sprinkle with the remaining breadcrumbs, leaving a couple of centimetres uncovered round the edge. Lay the apples and blackberries on top. Roll up and crimp the edges together. Brush with more melted butter. Transfer to a baking tray and cook in the oven for about 45 minutes, brushing occasionally with melted butter.

Serve warm, with icing sugar and crème fraîche.

This strudel is made in northern Italy during the blackberry season, and makes a delicious alternative to the well-known apple strudel

RICCIARELLI

Go into any bar in Siena and you will see ricciarelli neatly piled on plates, ready to buy individually. They are incredibly sweet, a creamy almond meringue dusted with icing sugar.

Makes 20 biscuits

300g blanched almonds

225g sugar

½ a lemon, zested

2 large free-range organic egg whites

½ teaspoon vanilla extract

½ teaspoon almond extract

icing sugar, for dusting

Preheat the oven to 160°C and roast the almonds for about 15 minutes, removing them from the oven just as they start turning brown. Leave the oven switched on and set the almonds aside to cool.

Blitz the roasted almonds, half the sugar and all the lemon zest in a food processor, until very fine. Whisk the egg whites until stiff, then beat in the remaining sugar and fold in the ground almond mixture along with the vanilla and almond extracts.

Dampen your hands, then take half a dessertspoon of mixture, roll it into a ball and flatten until about 2cm thick. Make about 20 of these, placing them on a baking tray lined with baking parchment and making sure there is at least 2.5cm space between the biscuits.

Bake in the oven for about 20–25 minutes, or until golden. Allow to cool on the tray, then remove and dust with icing sugar.

FLORENTINES

Makes 16

25g unsalted butter

80g caster sugar

75g glacé cherries, sliced

75g glacé ginger, chopped

100g flaked almonds

25g double cream

200g chocolate, 70% cocoa solids

Preheat the oven to 150°C.

Melt the butter and add the sugar. Bring to the boil, cook for 2 minutes, then remove from the heat, add the cherries, ginger and almonds and mix well. Stir in the cream.

Place the mixture in small heaps on 2 baking sheets lined with baking parchment, allowing room for them to spread. You should have room for 8 Florentines on each tray.

Bake in the oven until golden. Remove from the oven and, while still hot, pull the edges in and neaten the shape with a biscuit cutter. Leave on the baking sheet until cold.

Put the chocolate into a bowl over a pan of simmering water and leave until just melted. Dip each biscuit into the warm chocolate to thickly coat half only, and leave on a sheet of baking parchment until the chocolate sets hard. Serve the day you make them or the following day, as Florentines do not stay fresh.

CASTAGNACCIO

CHESTNUT PANCAKE

Castagnaccio is a Tuscan speciality made from October to Christmas, when the fresh chestnuts have just been harvested. Eat it when it is still warm and slightly crispy as a mid-morning snack, with a glass of spumanti secco, as they do in the bar at the Antonori Villa café on Via Tornabuoni in Florence.

Makes 2 large pancakes, roughly 30cm in diameter

500ml full-fat milk

500ml water

400g chestnut flour, sieved

4 heaped tablespoons caster sugar

1 teaspoon coarse sea salt, plus a little extra

100ml extra virgin olive oil, plus extra for the tin

100g raisins, soaked for at least 30 minutes in water or a glass of vin santo

50g pine nuts

a sprig of fresh rosemary, leaves picked

Preheat the oven to 220°C.

Put the milk and water into a large bowl and, using a large whisk, slowly add the flour, whisking to make a thin batter. Add the sugar, salt and olive oil and leave for 30 minutes in a warm place for the flour to expand.

Drain the raisins. Grease a large flat 30cm ovenproof pan or a non-stick frying pan that will fit in the oven. Pour in half the batter – it should be about 0.5cm deep. Scatter over half the pine nuts, raisins and rosemary leaves, drizzle with extra virgin olive oil, scatter over a little sea salt, and bake in the oven for 35–40 minutes, or until crispy at the edge and soft in the middle.

Make a second pancake using the rest of the ingredients – if you have 2 pans you can make both at the same time.

Always serve castagnaccio warm, cut into wedges, and as a snack rather than a cake.

ZABAGLIONE

For years we have been making zabaglione as an ice cream. Though it is more conventional, we are including this classic zabaglione in this chapter as it is both quick to make and delicious to eat. Use only the freshest organic eggs.

For 8

6 large free-range organic egg yolks

100g caster sugar

120ml dry Marsala

Place the egg yolks and sugar in a bowl that will rest easily on top of a pan. With a whisk or electric mixer, beat the yolks and sugar until they are pale yellow.

Fill the pan with water to half or three-quarters of the way up – the bowl, when placed on top, must not touch the water – and bring to the boil, then lower the heat to a gentle simmer. Put the bowl on top of the pan and add the Marsala, beating constantly for at least 15 minutes, or until the mixture forms soft peaks.

Spoon the zabaglione into Martini or wine glasses and serve immediately, with biscotti.

MONTE BIANCO

This celebration dish is very popular at Christmas and New Year. This recipe is for a large mountain. Source good-quality, rich chocolate — Green and Black's or the Italian Amadei 8 are excellent.

For 10–12

600g fresh chestnuts
1 litre full-fat milk
100g caster sugar
3 vanilla pods, split open lengthways
100g bittersweet chocolate, 85% cocoa solids, plus 50g extra for the plate
250ml double cream
100g icing sugar

Use a small sharp knife to score each chestnut on the rounded side. Place the chestnuts in a small pan and cover with cold water. Bring to the boil for 1 minute, then remove the pan from the heat. As soon as the chestnuts are cool enough to touch – they must not be cold, otherwise the skin will not come off – take them out of the pan one by one and peel off the outer and inner skins. Discard any discoloured bits. Keep the water warm; you may have to return it to the heat now and again with this quantity of chestnuts.

Place the peeled chestnuts in a pan and cover with the milk. Add the caster sugar and 2 of the vanilla pods. Bring to the boil, then simmer gently for 30 minutes, or until the chestnuts are soft. The milk should reduce and become slightly thicker. Test for sweetness and allow to cool.

Grate the chocolate finely. Drain the chestnuts, reserving the liquid. Put the chestnuts through a fine mouli to form a thick dough, or pulse in a food processor, then stir in the chocolate and enough of the milk to slightly loosen the mixture so that it will go easily through a piping bag fitted with a 2.5 or 3mm nozzle. Pipe it into a mountain on a large flat serving plate. The dough comes out of the nozzle quite slowly, so it will take time to form a good peak. Keep back the last 5cm of dough.

Cut the remaining vanilla pod in half and scrape out the seeds. Whisk the cream with the icing sugar until stiff, then add the vanilla seeds and stir well. Spoon the cream over the top of the chestnut mountain and pipe the remaining chestnut purée over to form craggy paths. Grate the remaining 50g of chocolate over the mountain base and the plate. Keep in a cold place, but not the fridge, until you want to serve it. Remember Monte Bianco doesn't keep for more than a few hours.

CANTUCCINI

In Tuscany, these biscuits are usually served with a glass of vin santo. Dipping the biscuits into the vin santo is not what the winemakers want you to do, though – rather, they want you to enjoy the contrast between the hard nutty crisp biscuits and the powerfully concentrated sweet golden wine.

Makes 30 biscuits

250g whole blanched almonds

100g unsalted butter, softened

150g caster sugar

3 large free-range organic eggs

200g plain flour

1 teaspoon baking powder

50g blanched almonds, ground to a flour

2 lemons, washed and zested

150g peeled hazelnuts

Preheat the oven to 150°C. Place the whole almonds on a baking tray and roast briefly until light brown. Remove from the oven and leave to cool.

Put the softened butter in a mixing bowl and add the sugar and the eggs. Lightly mix together, then sieve in the flour and baking powder. Mix to a thick dough, then fold in the almond flour and lemon zest. Add the roasted whole almonds and the hazelnuts, and stir to distribute them throughout the dough. Divide the dough into three and shape each piece into a 5 x 20cm flattened sausage.

Line a flat baking tray with greaseproof paper. Carefully lay on the three dough pieces, leaving a little space around each to allow for expansion. Place in the oven and bake for 15–20 minutes; the dough should be just cooked through and lightly golden. Leave to cool. When cool, place on a board and cut the dough across into 1.5cm width biscuits.

Lay the cut cantuccini back on the tray, cut side up, and put back into the oven to bake until they are a rich, deeper colour, and are dry and crisp. Then turn over and colour the other side. They will take up to 15 minutes on each side. Remove from the tray and cool on a rack. Serve with a glass of vin santo or a scoop of Marsala ice cream (see page 337).

SAUCES & STOCKS

SAUCES & STOCKS

We make Italian sauces every day at the River Café. How and when we serve them will depend on the fish, vegetable or meat we are cooking, or on a classic pairing. For instance, bollito misto is always served with a green sauce – either salsa verde or dragoncello (tarragon sauce) – and puntarelle, the salad of chicory shoots from Rome, requires a salted anchovy, vinegar and olive oil dressing. In Venice carpaccio is traditionally served with mustard mayonnaise lightly drizzled over.

As most Italian sauces are based on green herbs, the addition of ingredients such as anchovies, capers and good red wine vinegar are essential for adding saltiness, depth and complexity. We use only anchovies preserved in salt, and the best come from the Cantabrian Sea, off the coast of northern Spain. In Italy, cooks buy only as many anchovies as they need, ones sold by weight out of large five-kilo or ten-kilo tins.

Capers are the small unopened buds of a plant that grows wild throughout the Mediterranean and those from the island of Pantelleria are considered the best. Before using salted capers, soak them in water for ten minutes, rinse them in a sieve under running water and add a few drops of red wine vinegar.

Each region has its own traditional sauces. Bagna cauda comes from Piedmont, close to France, and is a rich garlic and anchovy sauce. We first ate it in a small trattoria in Barolo one November, so we make a version in the winter months, using red wine. The seasonal vegetables eaten with it were cardoons, artichokes and carrots. Pesto is the famous sauce historically made only in Liguria – it is used in most of the local pasta dishes, as well as in potato gnocchi and minestrone.

Bollito misto, the dish of mixed cooked meats from Emilia Romagna, is one of the rare dishes with which Italians serve more than one sauce – along with the traditional green sauces you might also have a salsa rosso and a fresh horseradish sauce. Horseradish sauce in Italy is less acidic than in other cuisines, as the addition of bread and olive oil masks the taste of the vinegar. In our version we add crème fraîche. It is important when buying horseradish to look for a root that is clean, firm and free from cuts and blemishes. When peeled, the root should be creamy white; the whiter the root the fresher it is. Fresh horseradish loses its pungent flavour rapidly, so make the sauce just before eating and in small amounts.

Slow-cooked tomato sauce is both the simplest sauce to make and one of the most difficult to get right. We make this sauce in the summer with fresh plum tomatoes and in the winter with tomatoes from jars. San Marzano are the fleshy, seedless, juiceless variety grown in southern Italy specifically for making tomato sauce. As they are grown only outside in the sun, they have a unique sweetness of flavour.

The stocks in this chapter are light and achieved by simply but carefully simmering chicken, veal or beef with celery, carrots, onion and parsley for about two hours. A flavourful vegetable broth, which can be used as an alternative to traditional meat and chicken broths, can be made by boiling seasonal vegetables such as carrots, celery, tomatoes, fennel, leeks, onions and herbs for about an hour.

In Italy nearly all these sauces are served in small quantities, enhancing, rather than overpowering, the fish, meat or vegetable. And a dish may be so perfectly and simply cooked that all it requires as a sauce is a drizzle of extra virgin olive oil and fresh lemon juice. Every November, we go to Italy to choose the olive oil for the River Café. New olive oil that has been recently pressed is green in colour and has a unique, peppery flavour. We can never wait to get the oil back to the restaurant to use for simply pouring over the seasonal greens that coincide with the arrival of the oil, cavolo nero and cicorias. There is nothing better than to celebrate the new oil by simply drizzling over a grilled bruschetta.

We also choose olive oils that are as distinct but with a less powerful flavour which we use for grilled fish and meats. Olive oils vary from region to region; the oil from Liguria is best for pesto as it is a gentler, lighter flavour. In the south of Italy in Puglia and Sicily, the olive oil has a nuttier flavour as the olives have grown in a hot climate. When you buy olive oil, look for ones from a named estate, ideally showing the year on which it was pressed.

SAPA

SALSA PER PUNTARELLE

FRESH GRAPE SYRUP

Sapa is a sweetener made without sugar and is cooked, which reduces it to a very thick syrup. The sweetness comes from the sugar content of the grapes, and it works more successfully with ripe black grapes, though some varieties of white grapes also have a high sugar content. Watery table grapes won't make a successful sapa.

For 6

2.25kg black grapes
200ml red wine

Wash and de-stem the grapes, blend to a pulp using a liquidizer, and put into a container with a tight-fitting lid. Cover the pulp with clingfilm so that it is touching the surface, then seal with the lid. Refrigerate for 2 days. Strain through a fine sieve, pressing as much liquid as possible through, and scraping to include any fine pulp that has stuck to the underside. Discard the pulp left in the sieve.

Put the juice into a large thick-bottomed pan and bring to the boil. Turn the heat down to medium and cook until thickened and reduced to a syrup, stirring to prevent it burning on the bottom. This will take 20–30 minutes. The syrup will form large bursting bubbles when ready. Finally, add the wine, bring to the boil again and cook on a high heat for 10 minutes, until it is a thin syrup. Leave to cool, and store in sterilized bottles – it will keep for up to 6 months, or in the fridge for a week.

Use the sapa when roasting game birds, poured over pannacotta, or as an alternative to red wine when baking whole pears slowly in the oven, as the Venetians love to do.

PUNTARELLE SAUCE

Anchovies preserved in salt have a delicate, sweet flavour. The fillets, rinsed and seasoned with black pepper and chilli, are soaked in red wine vinegar to make the basis for this sauce. The Romans use it to dress puntarelle, the green chicory buds that appear in Italian markets at the end of the year and are served sliced finely, as a salad.

For 6

10 whole salted anchovies
3 tablespoons red wine vinegar
1 garlic clove
2 dried chillies
1 teaspoon freshly ground black pepper
extra virgin olive oil
juice of 1 lemon

Wash the anchovies under cold running water and pull away the flesh from the head back to the tail. Cut them into 1cm pieces and place them in a small bowl. Cover with the vinegar, and stir to allow the anchovies to begin to dissolve. Peel and chop the garlic very finely and add to the bowl with the crumbled chillies and the pepper. Leave for 15 minutes for the flavours to combine, then add about 4 tablespoons of olive oil and lemon juice to taste and stir with a fork. The final sauce will have pieces of anchovy in it that are visible in the salad – an important texture for this dish.

BAGNA CAUDA

HOT ANCHOVY BATH FOR POACHED VEGETABLES

Anchovies and lots of garlic are the basis of this famous sauce from the Piedmont region of Italy. When talking to lovers of bagna cauda, we discovered that the other ingredients that go into the sauce vary enormously from village to village. We learnt this delicious version from one of the most famous Barolo producers in the area.

For 6

10 whole salted anchovies
500ml Barolo or Nebbiolo wine
10 garlic cloves, peeled and roughly chopped
250g cold unsalted butter, cubed
freshly ground black pepper

Wash the anchovies under cold running water and pull away the flesh from the head back to the tail. Rinse each fillet and roughly chop them. Gently heat the wine in a small, thick-bottomed pan, then add the garlic and leave on a gentle simmer until the wine has reduced by half. This will take up to 30 minutes. As the garlic softens, stir to mash it into the wine (we use a potato masher).

Add the anchovies and continue to cook very gently for about 15 minutes, stirring to break them up into the sauce until the texture becomes creamy. Finally, add the butter bit by bit, using a small whisk, and remove from the heat. The butter will thicken the sauce, which should be dark red and creamy in consistency. Season with black pepper.

Serve with a selection of hot poached vegetables, such as whole carrots, broccoli spears, artichokes, leeks, fennel and pumpkin segments, and Swiss chard stalks and leaves. Serve the vegetables in warmed bowls, with the bagna cauda spooned over.

SALSA D'ACCIUGHE E ROSMARINO

ANCHOVY AND ROSEMARY SAUCE

This is a sauce that goes particularly well with grilled fish. We have been making it at the River Café since we first opened, and the recipe developed out of a love of rosemary, which we grow all year round in our garden.

For 6

10 whole salted anchovies
1 lemon, juiced
1 tablespoon fresh rosemary leaves
freshly ground black pepper
6 tablespoons extra virgin olive oil

Finely chop the anchovies and put them into a bowl. Stir the lemon juice into the anchovies to 'melt' them. Chop the rosemary as finely as you can, then stir into the anchovies and season with black pepper. Finally, add the olive oil and mix well.

It is important to add the ingredients in this order and to use the sauce immediately, as the rosemary will oxidize very quickly and go black, spoiling the flavour.

SALSA VERDE

GREEN SAUCE

Salsa verde is one of the most basic and well known of the Italian green sauces. The following recipe is for a classic salsa verde, but it can be adjusted to your taste, or varied depending on the herbs in season. One of the pleasures of making salsa verde is in not making it uniform, but taking it step by step, which is not possible if you use a food processor. Instead, we use a mezzaluna.

For 6

4 tablespoons finely chopped fresh flat-leaf parsley leaves

3 tablespoons finely chopped fresh basil leaves

2 tablespoons finely chopped fresh mint leaves

extra virgin olive oil

2 tablespoons salted capers, rinsed in a sieve under cold water

6 anchovy fillets, either salted ones, rinsed, or tinned in oil

1 garlic clove, peeled

sea salt and freshly ground black pepper

1 tablespoon Dijon mustard

2 tablespoons red wine vinegar

Put the finely chopped herbs into a bowl and add 3 tablespoons of olive oil. Separately chop the capers and anchovies and stir into the herbs. Crush the garlic clove with a pinch of sea salt until smooth and add to the bowl. Finally stir in the mustard and vinegar and loosen the sauce with the olive oil, adding enough to make it quite runny. Season with black pepper.

SALSA DI DRAGONCELLO

TARRAGON SAUCE

Bollito misto is the famous dish of mixed boiled meats made by cooks in Emilia-Romagna. The dish is always served with a variety of sauces. Tradition is that at least one of these sauces is made with tarragon, the others usually being horseradish and chilli.

For 6

½ a ciabatta loaf, crusts removed

65ml red wine vinegar

3 large hard-boiled free-range organic egg yolks

6 salted anchovy fillets, finely chopped

50g salted capers, rinsed and finely chopped

3 tablespoons finely chopped fresh tarragon leaves

120–175ml extra virgin olive oil (although you may not need to use this much)

sea salt and freshly ground black pepper

Tear the bread into pieces and put into a bowl. Add the vinegar, cover with about 200ml of cold water and leave to soak for 20 minutes, until completely soft and mushy. Remove the bread from the water and squeeze out the excess liquid, then chop, ideally with a mezzaluna on a board.

Roughly break up the egg yolks with a fork, so that you have some bigger bits of yolks as well as some mashed.

Place the bread in a bowl, add the anchovies and capers, and mix thoroughly. Stir in the tarragon and, at the same time, add the olive oil slowly to loosen the sauce. Finally fold in the egg yolks, but not too much, stirring at this point so that you can still see the egg. Check for seasoning – you may only need to add pepper.

SALMORIGLIO

MARJORAM SAUCE

To make salmoriglio it really is essential to use a pestle and mortar, for it is in the crushing of the marjoram with the sea salt that the intense flavour is achieved. We use this sauce on scallops, monkfish and lobster, as its salty lemon flavour cuts the dense richness of these fish.

For 6

4 level tablespoons fresh marjoram leaves

1 teaspoon sea salt

2 tablespoons lemon juice

8 tablespoons extra virgin olive oil

freshly ground black pepper

In a pestle and mortar pound the marjoram leaves with the salt until completely crushed. Add the lemon juice, then slowly pour in the oil. Add a little pepper.

Variation: Fresh oregano, thyme or lemon thyme can be substituted for the marjoram.

SALSA CALDA DI OLIVE

HOT OLIVE AND CAPER SAUCE

This recipe comes from the restaurant U Giancu, near Rapallo, where Fausto, the owner, follows the Ligurian tradition, combining olives, capers and anchovies with a surprising twist that includes cream. We always serve it hot. It's pungent and creamy and a very unusual complement for steak.

For 6

250ml extra virgin olive oil

300g small Ligurian black and green Taggiasca olives, preserved in brine, pitted and rinsed

10 salted anchovy fillets, rinsed and roughly chopped

3 tablespoons salted capers, rinsed well under cold water and roughly chopped

2 garlic cloves, peeled and very finely chopped

150ml double cream

freshly ground black pepper

Heat the olive oil in a small pan until very hot. Add the olives, anchovies, capers and garlic. Cook for 2 minutes, stirring, just to soften the garlic, then remove from the heat, allow to cool briefly, and add the cream, stirring gently as the sauce thickens. Season with black pepper.

SALSA DI POMODORO CRUDO

RAW TOMATO SAUCE

In the summer, when the tomatoes are ripe and delicious, we make this sauce, which requires no cooking, to serve over ravioli or with spaghetti. It's best to make it a few hours before serving so that the tomatoes absorb the vinegar and garlic and the flavours combine.

For 6

300g ripe plum tomatoes

2 tablespoons red wine vinegar

1 tablespoon sea salt

100g ripe cherry tomatoes

4 garlic cloves, peeled

extra virgin olive oil

a small sprig of fresh basil, leaves picked

freshly ground black pepper

Slash down the length of each plum tomato. Plunge them into a pan of boiling water, leave for 10 seconds, then remove with a slotted spoon and drop them into a bowl of iced water to cool. Slip off the skins, halve each tomato and cut away the core. Chop roughly – you may lose a bit of the juice. Place in a bowl, sprinkle with the vinegar and half the sea salt and leave for 30 minutes.

Cut the cherry tomatoes in half and then in half again. As you cut them, squeeze out the juice and as many seeds as possible. Add the cherry tomato flesh to the plum tomatoes. Squash the garlic cloves to a fine paste with the rest of the sea salt. Stir into the tomatoes. Finally add 3–4 tablespoons of extra virgin olive oil and the basil leaves, torn into pieces.

SALSA ROSSA CRUDA

RAW TOMATO SAUCE WITH CHILLIES

Though we mostly accompany our meats and fish with the 'green sauces' – salsa verde, salmoriglio, salsa d'erbe, salsa di dragoncello – we think this sauce is delicious, particularly with grilled meats. The use of bread and vinegar with ripe tomatoes makes a substantial and piquant sauce for pork and veal chops in particular.

For 6

½ a ciabatta loaf

8 large ripe plum tomatoes

2 fresh red chillies

1 tablespoon dried oregano

sea salt and freshly ground black pepper

1½ tablespoons red wine vinegar

extra virgin olive oil

Preheat the oven to 150°C. Remove the crust from the ciabatta and tear the loaf into pieces. Place the pieces in a food processor and pulse-chop to largish crumbs. Place 3 tablespoons of the crumbs on a baking tray and dry them out in the oven for 15 minutes.

Skin the tomatoes (see previous recipe). Cut them in half, squeeze out the seeds and chop the flesh to a pulp. Cut the chillies in half lengthways, scrape out the seeds and finely chop. Mix the tomato pulp with the chillies and stir in the oregano. Add the breadcrumbs and season. Mix in the vinegar and add enough olive oil to make a thick sauce. Check again for seasoning.

RICH TOMATO SAUCE

This is quite simply one of the true classics of Italian cooking. With only four ingredients – tomato, onion, basil and garlic – it is one of the simplest sauces to make, yet the hardest with which to achieve a good result. It is crucial that you cook the onions gently and for as long as it takes them to 'melt' so that they disappear into the tomato sauce. Use as a pasta sauce, on an antipasti plate, or combined with vegetables such as green beans or cima di rape. It takes time and care to make. Use only Italian peeled plum tomatoes and look for ones packed in their own juice, not pulp. If you can only find them in pulp, be sure to drain them before using.

For 6

3 tablespoons extra virgin olive oil

3 red onions, peeled and sliced as finely as possible

2 garlic cloves, peeled and finely sliced

2 x 400g tinned or jarred whole Italian plum tomatoes, drained

sea salt and freshly ground black pepper

a small sprig of fresh basil, leaves picked

Heat the olive oil in a wide thick-bottomed pan over a medium heat. Add the onions and cook very gently for about 15 minutes, until very soft but not brown. Add the garlic and cook for a further 5 minutes or so, to allow it to cook into the onion completely. When the mixture begins to colour, add the tomatoes and stir to break them up, which will assist the amalgamation of the sauce. Season with sea salt and black pepper.

Cook slowly over a low heat, stirring occasionally, for 45 minutes or until you have a thick sauce. Tear up the basil and stir into the sauce. Check again for seasoning.

HORSERADISH SAUCE

Fresh horseradish is a common ingredient in northern Italy, usually combined with bread soaked in vinegar to accompany meats, particularly boiled meat. Traditionally a simple dry sauce that is extremely pungent, we add crème fraîche to make it lighter and sweeter.

For 6

100g fresh horseradish

1 tablespoon white wine vinegar

juice of ½ a lemon

sea salt and freshly ground black pepper

250ml crème fraîche

Peel the horseradish and grate it on the fine part of a cheese grater, then chop with a sharp knife to a fine pulp. Add the vinegar and lemon juice, season, and stir in half the crème fraîche. The sauce should be thick and not too creamy – taste for strength, then add as many more spoons of crème fraîche as you need to suit your taste.

FONDUTA PIEMONTESE

RICH CHEESE SAUCE FROM PIEDMONT

In Piemonte in October and November this wonderfully rich combination of eggs and cheese is found on many a menu. The triumph of this dish is the shavings of white truffles that cover the surface when the plate is presented to you.

For 4–5

300g Fontina cheese (or Asiago or other northern Italian melting mountain cheese), cut into 1cm cubes

150ml milk, or enough to just cover the cheese

100g unsalted butter, cut into pieces

4 large free-range organic egg yolks

Put the cheese into a bowl that will fit tightly over a medium pan and cover with the milk. Leave to soak for at least 1 hour in a warm place.

Half fill the pan with water and bring to a simmer. Turn the heat down to low, then place the bowl with the cheese mixture over the pan so that it sits snugly on top. The bottom of the bowl should not touch the simmering water.

Add the butter and heat very slowly, stirring, until the cheese is combined with the milk to make a creamy sauce. Add the egg yolks, one by one, beating them into the sauce but keeping the heat low, so as to just combine the eggs with the melted cheese, not cook them. If the sauce gets too hot, it will split.

This sauce is nearly always served with soft polenta, and in season white truffles are shaved generously over the plate. In Piemonte we have been served the fonduta by itself in a bowl, with, of course, the truffles generously shaved over.

FONDUTA DI PARMIGIANO

RICH PARMESAN SAUCE

In northern Italy this rich cheese sauce is served with boiled cardoons, the celery-like vegetable that tastes like artichokes. This combination is a passion of the Piedmontese.

For 6

1 garlic clove, peeled and crushed with a knife but kept whole

400ml crème fraîche

200g Parmesan cheese, grated

2 large free-range organic egg yolks

sea salt and freshly ground black pepper

Use a metal bowl that will fit inside a medium pan, leaving enough room to half fill the pan with water. Pour in the water and bring to a light simmer.

Rub the crushed garlic round the surface of the metal bowl. Add the crème fraîche, Parmesan and egg yolks. Place the bowl over the hot water and, whisking gently all the time, cook until the sauce thickens, about 15–20 minutes. Do not rush – a low heat is essential or the sauce will split. Season with salt and pepper and keep warm.

Use as a sauce for fresh tagliatelle cooked with thinly sliced asparagus, and serve immediately with freshly grated Parmesan. Alternatively, pour over baked polenta served with a slice of prosciutto or, as we discovered in Piedmont, over boiled cardoons.

SALSA PER CARPACCIO

PESTO

MUSTARD SAUCE FOR CARPACCIO

This sauce is inseparable from the carpaccio we have eaten in Venice. It is basically a mayonnaise thinned out with a small amount of milk and mustard, and should be liquid enough to drizzle lightly over the carpaccio.

For 6–8

1 large free-range organic egg yolk

juice of 1 lemon

300ml extra virgin olive oil

sea salt and freshly ground black pepper

1 tablespoon Worcestershire sauce

½ teaspoon Tabasco

1 tablespoon Dijon mustard

3 tablespoons milk

Put the egg yolk into a bowl and add 1 tablespoon of lemon juice. Beat with a whisk until amalgamated, then slowly add the olive oil, dribble by dribble. When the mayonnaise becomes stiff, add a little more lemon juice to loosen, then continue to add the remainder of the oil. Season with salt and pepper, then stir in the Worcestershire sauce and Tabasco. Finally, mix the mustard with the milk and stir into the mayonnaise – it should be the consistency of thick cream. Use a little extra milk to loosen if you feel the sauce is too thick.

When making pesto, choose the smaller, younger basil leaves – they have a sweeter taste and a softer texture, so they blend easily in a pestle and mortar. Basil from Liguria is famous worldwide for its flavour and perfume.

For 10–12

100g pine kernels

1 small garlic clove, peeled

sea salt

500g fresh basil leaves, washed and dried

200ml extra virgin olive oil

60g Pecorino Romano, freshly grated

40g Parmesan, freshly grated

Pound the pine kernels as finely as possible using a pestle and mortar. Remove from the mortar and set aside.

Now add the garlic to the mortar with 1 teaspoon of salt and grind to a fine paste. Add half the basil and pound it into the garlic until it becomes liquid. Continue to add the remaining basil leaves, a few at a time, until you have a thickish paste. Immediately add the pine kernels and 50ml of olive oil. Mix together with a spoon, not the pestle; the mixture will be quite dry at this point. Finally, add the Pecorino and Parmesan and enough oil to achieve a thick, creamy consistency. Check for seasoning.

Pesto keeps for about 2 months in jars in the fridge; pour over enough of the remaining oil to cover the surface and seal.

CHICKEN STOCK

Makes 2 litres

1 whole free-range chicken, cut into 4 or 5 pieces, fat and some of the skin removed

1 red onion, peeled and halved

2 medium carrots, peeled

4 celery stalks, halved

2 garlic cloves, peeled

a few fresh flat-leaf parsley stalks

5 black peppercorns

3 bay leaves or sprigs of fresh thyme

sea salt

Put all the ingredients, except the salt, into a large pan and cover with 2–3 litres of cold water. Bring to the boil, skimming off the scum as it comes to the surface, then lower the heat and simmer very gently for 1½ hours.

Strain, season with salt and leave to cool. If you are not using it immediately, the stock will keep in the refrigerator for up to 2 days.

VEAL STOCK

Makes 2 litres

3 veal shin or knuckle bones

1 red onion, peeled and halved

2 medium carrots, peeled

4 celery stalks, halved

2 garlic cloves, peeled

a few fresh flat-leaf parsley stalks

5 black peppercorns

3 bay leaves or sprigs of fresh thyme

sea salt

Preheat the oven to 180°C. Put the veal bones on a baking tray and roast in the oven for 40 minutes. Deglaze the tray with a little boiling water, scraping up any caramelized juices from the bottom.

Put the bones, the roasting juices and all the other ingredients except the salt into a large pan. Cover with 2.5–3 litres of cold water and bring to the boil, skimming off the scum as it comes to the surface. Lower the heat and simmer very gently for up to, but no more than, 2 hours.

Strain, season with salt and leave to cool. If you are not using it immediately, the stock will keep in the refrigerator for up to 2 days.

Note: for a light veal stock it is not necessary to roast the bones first.

BRODO DI PESCE

FISH STOCK

The best fish stock is made from the bones of a turbot, but monkfish and halibut bones have a sweet flavour too. Ask your fishmonger if he can give you some of these.

Makes 2 litres

bones, fins and tail of 1 large turbot, halibut or monkfish
2 red onions, peeled and cut into quarters lengthways
2 carrots, sliced
4 celery stalks, halved
a few fresh flat-leaf parsley stalks
6 white or black peppercorns
2 bay leaves
1 fennel bulb, untrimmed, cut in half
sea salt

Put all the ingredients except the salt into a large pan, cover with about 2 litres of cold water and bring to the boil, skimming off the scum as it comes to the surface. Lower the heat and simmer gently for 15–20 minutes; in order to achieve a fresh-tasting stock, do not be tempted to simmer for longer than this. Check for seasoning and add sea salt if necessary. Strain and use immediately.

BRODO DI VERDURA

VEGETABLE STOCK

Makes 2 litres

2 tablespoons olive oil
2 small red onions, peeled and roughly sliced
4 carrots, halved
1 head of celery, stalks and leaves, cut lengthways in four
4 leeks, tough green tops removed, halved
2 fennel bulbs, each cut into four
2 dried red chillies
4 garlic cloves, peeled
1 x 15g packet of fresh thyme
1 x 60g packet of fresh flat-leaf parsley, leaves and stalks separated
2 litres water
4 bay leaves
2 tablespoons white or black peppercorns
juice of 1 lemon
sea salt

Heat the oil in a large heavy-bottomed pan and gently fry the onions for about 5 minutes until soft. Add the carrot, celery, leeks and fennel, and fry for another 5 minutes or so, stirring, until lightly browned. Add the chillies, garlic, thyme and parsley leaves, stir to combine and continue to cook for 2 or 3 minutes, stirring regularly. Add the water, parsley stalks, bay leaves and peppercorns, and bring to the boil. Lower the heat and simmer gently for about 1 hour before straining. Add the lemon juice and adjust the seasoning.

DRESSINGS

The dressings we make, which highlight the flavours of fresh interesting salad leaves, are made with carefully chosen single estate extra virgin olive oil, good-flavoured red wine vinegar or fresh lemon juice, sea salt and freshly ground black pepper. The basic proportions we adhere to are four parts olive oil to one part lemon or vinegar. In the River Café we dress each salad before serving, but at home, we do what they do in Italy – just put the olive oil and vinegar or lemon on the table and let everyone dress their own.

OIL AND LEMON DRESSING

For 6
juice of 2 lemons
extra virgin olive oil
sea salt and freshly ground black pepper

Mix the lemon juice with four times its volume of extra virgin olive oil. Season with salt and pepper and toss with your salad leaves just seconds before serving.

OIL, LEMON AND BALSAMIC DRESSING

This is a dressing for bitter winter leaves and wild leaves. Traditional balsamic vinegar takes between twelve and forty years to make, being a slow ageing of wine and vinegar musk in a variety of small wooden barrels. It is made in only one region of Italy – Modena – and has its own DOC, requiring the final product to be bottled in a round bottle of particular dimensions. The wording on the bottle should include 'traditional', to be sure that it is the real thing.

For 6

100ml extra virgin olive oil

juice of 1 large lemon

sea salt and freshly ground black pepper

2 teaspoons aged thick balsamic vinegar

Mix the oil with the lemon juice, season, and pour over your salad leaves. Toss to coat each leaf, then drizzle over the balsamic vinegar. Serve immediately.

OIL, VINEGAR AND MUSTARD DRESSING

For 6

3 tablespoons Dijon mustard

100ml red wine vinegar

300ml extra virgin olive oil

sea salt and freshly ground black pepper

Put the mustard into a bowl. Stir in the vinegar and then very slowly add olive oil until it is the consistency of mayonnaise. Season to taste.

INDEX

The authors would like to thank **Chefs in Italy** Danny Bohan, James Fincham, Sophie Roche-Garland, Joseph Trevelli, and Ivana Fabbrizzi, Luigi Gianni, and all the River Café chefs and staff 2008–2009 **Photographers** Giuseppe Bartolini, Jonathan Gregson, David Loftus, Amedeo Novelli, Jean Pigozzi, Mark Read, Alan Rusbridger

Designers Sarah Habershon, Mark Porter **Penguin** Lindsey Evans, John Hamilton, Keith Taylor, Tom Weldon **And** Marilisa Allegrini, David Gleave, Dante MacIlwaine-Gray, Ossie Gray, Ian Heide, Annie Lee, Georgina Levy, Tanya Nathan, Bren Parkins-Knight, Jess Shadbolt, Ed Victor, David MacIlwaine, Richard Rogers

OUR FAVOURITE PLACES

CAMPANIA

Il Ceppo (restaurant)
Via Madonna del Carmine 31,
84043 Agropoli
www.hotelristoranteilceppo.
com
Tel 0974 843036

Lo Scoglio (restaurant)
Piazza delle Sirene 15,
Marina del Cantone
081 8081026

LAZIO

Albergo Ristorante Adriano
(hotel and restaurant)
Via di Villa Adriana 222,
Tivoli, 00010 Rome
www.hoteladriano.it
0774 535028

La Carbonara
(restaurant)
Piazza Campo de' Fiori 23,
00186 Rome
www.la-carbonara.it
06 6864783

Piperno (restaurant)
Monte de Cenci 9, 00186 Rome
www.ristorantepiperno.com
06 68806629

Puntarossa Da Renatone
(restaurant)
Via dei Monti dell'Ara,
Maccarese, 00057 Fumicino,
Rome
www.renatone.net
06 6672300

LIGURIA

Gianni Franzi (restaurant)
Piazza Marconi 5,
19018 Vernazza
www.giannifranzi.it
0187 821003

Trattoria Da Laura
(trattoria; by foot or boat from
Portofino or Camogli)
Via San Fruttuoso, San
Fruttuoso, 16032 Camogli
0185 772589

LOMBARDY

Da Giacomo (restaurant)
Via Pasquale Sottocorno 6,
20129 Milan
02 76023313

Dal Bolognese
(restaurant)
Piazza della Repubblica 13,
20124 Milan
02 62694843

La Latteria (trattoria)
Via San Marco 24-22/A,
20100 Milan
065 97653

PIEDMONT

Osteria Da Gemma (trattoria)
Via Marconi 6, 12050 Roddino
0173 794252

Osteria La Salita
(trattoria)
Via Marconi 2/A,
12065 Monforte d'Alba
0173 787196

PUGLIA

Il Poeta Contadino
(restaurant)
Via Indipendenza 21,
70011 Alberobello
www.ilpoetacontadino.it
080 4321917

TUSCANY

Alla Vecchia Bettola
(trattoria)
Via Luigi Ariosto 34r,
50100 Florence
055 224158

Antica Macelleria Cecchini
(butcher's shop
and restaurant)
Via XX Luglio 11,
50020 Panzano
055 852020

Bar Da Pietro (café)
Via Pieve 7a, Pieve di Camaiore,
55041 Camaiore
0584 9818466

**Caffè Giacosa by
Roberto Cavalli** (café)
Via della Spada 10,
50131 Florence
www.caffegiacosa.it
055 2776328

Cibreo (restaurant)
Via del Verrocchio 8r,
50122 Florence
055 2341100

Da Delfina
(restaurant)
Via della Chiesa 1,
59015 Artimino
www.dadelfina.it
055 8718074

Da Romano
(restaurant)
Via G. Mazzini 122,
55049 Viareggio
www.romanoristorante.it
0584 31382

Da Ruggero
(restaurant)
Via Senese 89,
50124 Florence
055 220542

Da Venanzio
(restaurant)
Piazza Palestro 3,
Colonnata di Carrara,
54030 Carrara
0585 758062

Le Panzanelle
(trattoria)
Loc. Lucarelli 29,
53017 Radda in Chianti
0577 733511

**Ristorante I Due
Cippi da Michele**
(restaurant)
Piazza Via Veneto 26,
58014 Saturnia
056 4601074

Tenuta di Capezzana
(wine producer
and cookery school)
Via Capezzana 100,
59015 Carmignano
www.capezzana.it
055 8706005

Trattoria Da Marino
(trattoria)
Via Provinciale Lucchese 102,
51030 Serravalle Pistoiese
0573 51042

VENETO

Al Pompiere
(trattoria)
Vicolo Regina d'Ungheria 5,
37121 Verona
www.alpompiere.com
045 8030537

Alle Testiere (restaurant)
Calle del Mondo Nuovo,
Castello 5801, San Lio,
30122 Venice
041 5227220

Bottega del Vino
(restaurant/enoteca)
Via Scudo di Francia 3,
37121 Verona
045 8004535

Caffè Filippini (café)
Piazza Erbe 26,
37121 Verona
www.caffefilippini.it
045 8004549

**Enoteca della
Valpolicella**
(wine shop and bar)
Via Osan 45, 37022 Fumane
045 6839146

Groto di Corgnan (restaurant)
Via Corgnan 41,
37010 Sant'Ambrogio
di Valpolicella
045 7731372

Harry's Bar
(restaurant)
Calle Vallaresso 1323,
30124 Venice
041 5285777

Trattoria Caprini
(trattoria; special
handmade pasta)
Via Paolo Zanotti 9,
Torbe di Negrar,
37024 Verona
045 7500511